More Praise for *More Than Money*

"More than a master of business administration, Mark Albion offers his readers an advanced degree in the meaning of life. His MBA is a Master of Blessed Attitude, and it suggests a course of personal development that will give everyone more than money—it will give them purpose, direction, and hope."

—Alan M. Webber, former editorial director and
managing editor, *Harvard Business Review*

"Dr. Albion has developed the tools for helping us find our way in our professional lives. While this book is written for MBAs, it will speak to anyone who has struggled to find more meaning in his or her career. A compelling writer, Dr. Albion is open about himself, admits his mistakes, and through his own telling of how he learned from them, teaches us how to recognize ours and change the course of our lives for the better."

—Phoebe Higgins, Dominican University of
California, MBA, 2007

"The basic messages of the book summon up, and resonate with, my own experiences as an MBA student, and I realize that I would have been one of the people this book was intended for. I'm reminded of some of the lessons I've learned the hard way since leaving my MBA program. Not only does *More Than Money* invite us to question how success is really best measured, but it also offers some practical tools for finding a more holistic return on an MBA investment."

—David Wood, Fisher Graduate School,
Monterey Institute, MBA, 1993

"Before getting an MBA, read *More Than Money*. This book revolutionizes business school education and will help any MBA student get more out of school. In his special way, Dr. Mark leads you to define first what you want to do with your life. He does so by guiding you not with answers but with crucial questions that help you connect with who you are and what you wanted as a child but deemed impossible. Now it is possible."

—Anton Arapetyan, Lviv (Ukraine) University
MBA, 2006, Lviv Business School

"*More Than Money* reaffirms that as human beings we first need to love and be loved—before we are MBAs. Our MBA degrees, our positions, money, and assets are tools that can help us to love. For when all is said and done, on our deathbeds, love is the only thing that will have mattered. Thank you, Dr. Mark, for being that voice that speaks to our spirits, not just our heads."

—Tolulope Ilesanmi, McGill University,
MBA, 2005

"This book has me thinking in a very serious way about my life, my place in the world, and how my strengths and talents can be of service. It has me remembering the best times at work and how good it felt to be working together toward common objectives with a common purpose and with passion. I'd like to find that again. *More Than Money* is really going to help me focus on doing so."

—Douglas Hammer, New York University, Stern
School of Business, MBA, 1999

"We have all heard stories of business school graduates who took decades to realize the careers they chose right out of school were the wrong ones for them. Benefit from the teachings in this book and start building yourself a sustainable career now, so you don't have to undo your mistakes later."

—Erika Haas, Stanford Graduate School of
Business, MBA, 1998

MORE THAN
MONEY

MORE THAN MONEY

QUESTIONS EVERY MBA NEEDS TO ANSWER

Redefining Risk and Reward for a Life of Purpose

Mark Albion

BK

Berrett–Koehler Publishers, Inc.
San Francisco
a BK Life book

Berrett-Koehler Publishers, Inc.
235 Montgomery Street, Suite 650
San Francisco, CA 94104-2916
Tel: (415) 288-0260   Fax: (415) 362-2512   www.bkconnection.com

Ordering Information

Quantity sales. Special discounts are available on quantity purchases by corporations, associations, and others. For details, contact the "Special Sales Department" at the Berrett-Koehler address above.

Individual sales. Berrett-Koehler publications are available through most bookstores. They can also be ordered directly from Berrett-Koehler: Tel: (800) 929-2929; Fax: (802) 864-7626; www.bkconnection.com

Orders for college textbook/course adoption use. Please contact Berrett-Koehler: Tel: (800) 929-2929; Fax: (802) 864-7626.

Orders by U.S. trade bookstores and wholesalers. Please contact Ingram Publisher Services, Tel: (800) 509-4887; Fax: (800) 838-1149; E-mail: customer.service@ingrampublisherservices.com; or visit www.ingrampublisherservices.com/Ordering for details about electronic ordering.

Berrett-Koehler and the BK logo are registered trademarks of Berrett-Koehler Publishers, Inc.

Printed in the United States of America

Berrett-Koehler books are printed on long-lasting acid-free paper. When it is available, we choose paper that has been manufactured by environmentally responsible processes. These may include using trees grown in sustainable forests, incorporating recycled paper, minimizing chlorine in bleaching, or recycling the energy produced at the paper mill.

Library of Congress Cataloging-in-Publication Data

Albion, Mark S., 1951-
       More than money : questions every MBA needs to answer / by Mark Albion.
          p. cm.
       ISBN 978-1-57675-656-0 (hbk. : alk. paper)
          1. Industrial management—Vocational guidance.   2. Career development.   I. Title.
HD38.2.A3473 2008
650.14--dc22   2008030281

First Edition
13 12 11 10 09 08   10 9 8 7 6 5 4 3 2 1

Project management, design, and composition by Dovetail Publishing Services.

To Joy,
for thirty years

▪ ▪ ▪ ▪ ▪ CONTENTS

■ ■ ■ ■ ■ FOREWORD

Liz Cutler Maw, Executive Director, Net Impact

"Incredible." "Dynamic." "Inspiring." "Awesome."

As MBAs, you encounter many kinds of teachers. There are tenured professors who recite lectures from memory. There are guest lecturers who bring real-live case studies into the classroom. There are patient tutors who symbolically hold your hand through the crunch of the core curriculum.

And then there is Mark Albion.

Mark is a different kind of teacher, one who ventures outside the classroom walls to teach what he loves to people he loves. Mark is passionate about finding meaning in life and work, and he has made it his life's mission to share that passion with others.

At the Net Impact annual conference, we are fortunate to see countless great speakers, but few have made the impact on students that Mark Albion has. The adjectives at the beginning of this section are just a few of the accolades heard yearly as we poll attendees on their favorite speakers. Mark's name is always at the top of that list.

Why is Mark such a hit with MBAs and other business students or professionals?

I have my theories:

► Mark embodies the advice he gives. *In More Than Money*, Mark advises readers to think differently about career possibilities. Mark's personal story is one in which he thought differently, chose differently, and acted differently—and he glows with personal peace from doing so.

► Mark understands that his topic is a hard one. It's not easy to make career choices during business school, with the many options, sources of advice, and financial constraints you face. Choosing the right job or internship can seem like the most important decision in the world to stressed and overwhelmed MBA students. Mark knows this, and he doesn't belittle the seriousness of the choice but rather supports his audience to make the decision the right way.

► Like any good student, Mark has done his homework. He has collected hundreds of life stories and examples of career paths, and he has traveled the globe to learn and share these experiences with others.

► Mark is warm, funny, and caring. It's much easier to believe everything will be OK with Mark as a guide instead of some of the other types you might meet on your MBA journey. (You know the types I mean.) And Mark's right—it will be OK! Especially if you use *More Than Money* as a resource.

At Net Impact, too often we hear from MBA students that they are torn about how to make a difference and when to make a change in their career. The decisions are tough ones, and the answers depend on each individual's passions, talents, and life goals. This book is for everyone who is pondering these issues now or who will face them in the future. Mark will lead you through his unique process of asking the right questions and finding the right path.

There are many books designed to get you thinking about your career and others that help you explore your feelings about your life, but very few intermingle the two as successfully as Mark has. *More Than Money* will ask you hard questions about who you are, what you want, and how you make decisions. If you challenge yourself, it may not be the easiest book you've ever read, but it may save you years of heartache.

Mark organizes his book around four questions and twelve lifelines, the result of which is what he terms a "destiny plan." He offers you choices on how deep you want to delve into the questions he poses and offers suggestions for working with groups of friends or colleagues to explore ideas and potential actions. He also offers tools and resources to equip you on your quest. And he throws in many great stories to keep you inspired and to make you smile. Whether you're curious and just want to enjoy Mark's readable prose or you're ready to get down to the details of planning your future, Mark's book will reward your efforts with new insights and possibilities.

This book is a gift from a dedicated friend of Net Impact and a devoted mentor for MBA students and professionals around the world. As Mark says, *More Than Money* "supports you to follow your dream and make a contribution." I hope that this book leads you not just to more than money but to a future that is more satisfying than you had ever dared to dream.

Liz Cutler Maw has been Net Impact's Executive Director since the fall of 2004. Liz has been active with the Net Impact network since 1999; she was a co-leader of the student Net Impact chapter at Columbia Business School and a co-founder and leader of the Bay Area Professionals Chapter. Liz's professional experience includes strategic consulting to nonprofits with the Bridgespan Group, a not-for-profit strategy consulting firm, as well as fundraising and direct marketing for nonprofit organizations in New York City and Washington, D.C. She holds a BA with honors from Yale University and an MBA from Columbia Business School. Liz also spent one semester at the Haas School of Business at U.C. Berkeley.

■ ■ ■ ■ ■ PREFACE

I don't know what your destiny will be, but one thing I know: the only ones among you who will be really happy are those who have sought and found how to serve.

Albert Schweitzer, humanitarian

When was the last time you were called an "arrogant asshole" and it led to a compliment?

I remember the last time it happened to me: December 16, 2002. Yes, someone really called me that to my face—in public, no less. And yes, she was right.

This public unmasking made me think more deeply about my life and career path than I had in my first fifty-one years. In reflection, I kept coming back to the central question of this book, the question that will help you begin your journey from business school to your unique destiny.

Over the past six years, this question has spawned other questions, many of which were posed by MBAs attending my speeches. Your "assignment" is to choose those questions that resonate most deeply with you and address them. They will help you think differently about your career and your place in the world. They will help you find your path of service, your personal path of happiness and fulfillment.

But first, let me tell you what happened that unusual winter day.

After the corporate embarrassments of the unethical activities of Enron, Tyco, WorldCom, and others, the Harvard Business School Alumni Association was not going to invite another CEO to speak at its 2002 year-end session. Instead, the alums decided to get someone "safe." They chose me.

xiii

I'd left Harvard in 1988 after nearly twenty years as a student and professor. I'd been back to school many times since then, speaking to various groups of students, large and small, about a network of service-minded MBAs I had cofounded, Net Impact, and its parent organization, Social Venture Network, the preeminent network of socially conscious entrepreneurs.

It was always fun to come back to speak at my old haunt—and a bit strange, too. Maybe I didn't act the same or speak the same as I did at the other business schools I'd visited. Whatever it was, something unusual always happened when I spoke at the institution that had been my "home" and my identity for the first half of my adult life.

I gave my speech to a packed hall of HBS graduates. It seemed to go well, I guess. I handed out my latest media effort, a three-CD series titled *Finding Work That Matters*, and asked for questions. Many hands shot up, and I chose one near me, in the first row. The hand, the person, looked familiar. I wasn't sure. Soon I would be.

"Thank you for coming, Professor Albion," she began. "My name is Sara Smith [not her real name]. I was one of your students in first-year marketing back in 1982."

Yes, I remembered her and drifted back twenty years in my mind. I tried hard to picture the thirty-one-year-old Professor Albion. Then came the wake-up call.

"May I say that while I think we learned a lot about marketing in your class that year, you were the most arrogant, self-centered asshole I had ever encountered in my life."

Thank you, Ms. Smith, I thought, for that announcement to yours truly *and* the audience. That should get me a speedy request to come back to speak to alums soon! Maybe I had given her a bad grade? Maybe not. But thankfully, there was more to come.

"And as much as you came across as a Mr. Know-It-All, and as much as your self-absorbed attitude and arrogance repelled me then, today I find you kind and gentle, a caring man, who has wisdom to share and has done so in an engaging, collaborative manner. Today, you seem to have as many questions as answers—a curiosity and wonder about life I find quite infectious. And you are so energetic and seem so happy! I don't know what happened in the last twenty years, Professor Albion, but you obviously learned a lot. Congratulations. Good for you!"

In the following weeks, I realized that Sara had described someone I no longer knew (I hoped!) but someone she had described accurately. Back in my Harvard days, despite my accomplishments, I felt insecure and ungrounded. I was in need of reconnecting with who I was, who I wanted to become, and what I was placed on earth to do. I was not yet on my *destiny path*.

Sara got me thinking about my destiny: If I died, how would I be remembered? What would my eulogy be? Would people remember me as the first person she described or as the second one? My reaction was simple: "I wish I had thought about this earlier in my career!"

More Than Money asks one question in many ways, using questions and stories to reframe your career decisions for life's essential purpose: *What will your contribution be?* The answer will tell you how you will be remembered, how future generations will think of you when they look at your ancestral tree, and when your eulogy is read, whether or not you'd be proud of what is said.

How paradoxical, you might say, that you start your career search by contemplating your death! Yet that is the key to developing a destiny plan—the key to living *your life*.

Beginning with the question of contribution rather than the more usual "How can I make a living?" makes all the difference in the path you'll choose and where you'll end up. It will give you a strong foundation for all that follows, implicitly changing your business focus from *getting* to *giving*. Your reward is that you've taken the first step toward managing your career with your heart, the pathway for great things to happen.

To answer this question of contribution, you'll need to consider how your work will fit into your life. Be aware that in death, rarely will loved ones remember you for your work in private enterprise as much as for what you've done for your family and contributed to civil society.

There is one caveat that is crucial to your ability to make that contribution when making your career choices: *What you perceive to be your "safest" choices may be your riskiest, and vice versa.* Reframing this mental and emotional shift, convincing you to make it, and supporting and guiding you to act on it in your own way—that is the work of this book.

More Than Money is meant to complement a business school education. Whereas a rapidly growing number of schools now have courses in sustainable development, microfinance, corporate social responsibility, and social enterprise, few have material to help you develop a *sustainable career*. The book is written so that whether you are considering business school, entering business school, a current student, or a graduate, it should speak directly to you. I know. I've sat in your seat.

Who Is Mark Albion?

I am a "conflicted achiever." Maybe you are, too.

Like many of you, I worked hard to get the best education I could find and then took the highest-paying, most prestigious job I could get to build a career platform from which I hoped to leap into work that I'd really love. What I found out is that it wasn't that simple and that there was a price to pay for taking that path. And I probably wouldn't have had to pay that price, even taking a similar path, if I had been more aware of who I was and what I really wanted.

The first half of my life was Harvard. I began Harvard College when I was fourteen years old. Not actually, of course, but it was true in *my* mind. I'd meet girls and tell them I went to Harvard to impress them. I thought they believed me. Maybe not. Maybe they did by the time I was sixteen. I don't know. I just know I didn't care back then. I knew that when the time came, I was going to Harvard, and that was that. There was never a question in my mind.

I'll bet you too have a "Harvard" in your life. "Harvard" represents reaching your dream, showing everyone how good you are, how accomplished you are, how special you are. It's society's confirmation that your life on earth counts—counts more than the lives of most other people.

I needed that confirmation, that identity. My parents divorced before I could remember, and I had barely seen my father. Maybe I thought that I was the reason for their breakup or the reason Dad rarely saw me. I don't know. But

I knew one thing: my mother loved me, and if I went to Harvard, my father would surely love me, too.

That's all I really wanted: to be loved. And respected, I might add. Everything else was simply a facsimile of this truth. Maybe that's your truth.

My father had gone to Harvard (he was even buried in 2007 wearing his Harvard Class of '45 tie). So in 1969, where else could I have gone to college? Dad picked my major (economics) and one of his real estate properties served as the basis for my undergraduate thesis. I felt that those choices would bring me closer to Dad, but my heart wasn't in it.

As graduation loomed, it was a slow period for selling real estate, so instead of going to school or working, I backpacked around the world for a year. It was a "socially unacceptable" choice, but it would be the most important experience of my young life.

I learned that I could take care of myself and that there were many ways to live a life. I learned about compassion, something lacking in my previous education. I worked with children in impoverished areas of India and the South Pacific. I supported myself by arranging an import-export business with Dad. It paid for the trip and made Dad good money, too.

Back home in the United States, however, I felt the irresistible attraction of Harvard once again. I visited the head of the joint business-economics doctoral program between Harvard Business School and the Graduate School of Arts and Sciences, Professor John Lintner. He dismissed me because my college grades were too low. But I refused to leave, returning each day, sitting outside his office, getting to know his secretary.

I did eventually get Professor Lintner to give me a chance: take a full load of his handpicked graduate economics courses for two semesters, he told me, and if I got all A's, he would consider my application for the following year.

I buckled down and worked harder than I had since high school. I lived six days a week in the library (I actually had a bed in the stacks). I had a lot of catching up to do. Catch up I did. That next spring, I received an acceptance letter for the joint PhD program. I still remember the moment as if it were yesterday. I cried, and cried some more. I'd won! What I had won I was not sure.

And then I broke down.

The next three weeks I was bedridden, exhausted and ill from seven months of nonstop work and pressure. But I was back at Harvard again, the way I wanted it to be. I had paid the price through tireless study and poor health for a few weeks—a trade for something I so deeply wanted that I was happy to make it. It was a trade to make me feel good and look good in the eyes of others. What I needed was to *be* good and *do* good.

I enjoyed my six years as a graduate student, including three years as an undergraduate economics adviser and instructor. I wrote a book and a few journal articles as well. But I struggled with values. In my graduate economics courses, we studied how to make markets work better, how to make the world a better place for all. At the business school, we studied how to make the market work in your company's favor, how to make the world a better place—for me. Public purpose versus private profit.

What did I do? I chose not to pay attention to my heart, my passion for market equity and social justice. When I finished my joint doctoral work, I didn't become an economics professor but instead became a professor at the business school—it paid better. I did enjoy the stimulating colleagues, motivated students, and seemingly limitless research and consulting opportunities. I made money beyond my expectations and even garnered my fifteen minutes of fame.

In many ways, the achiever in me loved it. But the conflict in me grew. Where was the person who had helped poor children in India in 1973? Where was the writer, the adviser, who wanted to help students create a life of contribution and fulfillment after college?

I would have to leave the business school in 1988 to pursue what I would later call my destiny. I couldn't articulate my destiny yet, but I knew what it wasn't. The defining moment came one evening on my way to the school parking lot to get my car and go home.

It was around 10:00 P.M. when I walked by the window of Professor Lintner's office. In my graduate school years, we had taught together and spent many hours discussing our mutual love of research. He had become my mentor. I looked up at that window and thought of the man who occupied it.

Here was a man I greatly respected, even loved. Here was a man at the top of his profession, a Nobel Prize winner, though he died before the award was given to his research colleagues. Here was a man who in my eyes had all the right values, turning down White House appearances if it meant canceling a class. I knew that if I did well, I could someday become a resident of that office.

I thought of my "contribution," my tombstone. I visualized my birth date, a spot for date of death, and that dash in between. How was I going to spend that dash? I wasn't sure, but I knew at that moment that occupying his office wasn't it! I would feel that I had spent my life in the wrong place. Why? I didn't exactly know. Where was the right place? I absolutely did not know.

In 1988, the second half of my life began, the Net Impact years of helping service-minded MBAs find their destiny path and in so doing helping Mark Albion find his own. These twenty years are captured in this book. Whereas I helped found small, socially responsible businesses, following in my mother's footsteps, I learned that I still loved teaching and research; I just needed to change subjects! The lessons learned from that transition are the foundation of *More Than Money.*

The Book: Why I Wrote It, How You Can Use It and Benefit from It

I wrote *More Than Money* for three reasons. The first is to make money and leave a legacy. Coincidentally, the book is an example of two key messages: money is an important goal, but so is serving yourself and others. When I made a lot of money, I probably gave too much away. Maybe I was out of balance. But I did what I thought was right and have few regrets. After giving probably too much of my time away as well to the three nonprofits I love—Net Impact, Social Venture Network, and Temple Beth David—it's time for me to provide for my family.

The second reason is to inspire you, to give you the courage to focus your career on service, on creating a better world for all. Given all of your educational opportunities, I believe that each of you has a lucky lottery ticket in life compared with the other 6.7 billion people on earth. You are all going to make a good living. The question is, what else will you do with that ticket? I want to help you use that ticket to serve others and in that way serve yourself.

The third reason is to provide you with a guidebook for what can be a difficult career path. After a school speech a decade ago, one of my best friends and colleagues, Deb Imershein, warned, "Mark, you do a great job of getting the MBAs all fired up. But then they go out and get shot!"

Today, organizations like Net Impact can help you develop a support community and get jobs that honor your values. But there's no personal guidebook. So think of *More Than Money* as a mirror to look at yourself—to examine your passions, goals, career, and life. It's something we all need help doing. The heart of the book, the four chapter title questions and twelve lifelines (described in the next section), takes you through the process of constructing what I've called a *destiny plan*, a plan to help you seek and find your unique "inner realizable purpose of life."

In addition to the four chapter title questions, there are sixty-four sets of questions to help you construct this personal, authentic plan: thirteen for each of the four chapters and four each at the end of the Preface, Introduction, and Conclusion. These questions appear at the end of the introductory section of each chapter and after each lifeline. You should use only those questions that work for you. No one is expected to use them all.

The questions in the Preface ask you to start off by thinking about where you want to end up (for example, what will your contribution be?). The Introduction follows by zooming in on today and your business school experience. Your responses give you an end point and a starting point to construct your plan as you read and respond to the next four chapters. The questions at the end of the Conclusion ask you to reach inside and outside further, if you can.

You will see my destiny description, the core of your plan, without specific timetables and the like, in Chapter 1. You will see a structure that works for me, but there is no one format for a description, much less a plan. It is a work in progress structured to be most useful to you. Its level of detail depends on how you use the book.

Depending on how much time you have and what benefits you are looking for, there are at least three ways you can use this book.

1. *For inspiration.* Read the book, taking notes on what questions and challenges strike you as most compelling. Then return to those sections, reread the relevant stories and discussion, and come up with changes you think you need to make. Put one into action in your next job search.

2. *For courage.* Skim the book and then read in detail the sections that most interest you with a group of friends. Discuss your different paths and reactions, gathering ideas of how you might support each other in making changes.

3. *As a guide.* Use the entire book as a workbook. Read through it once, and then go back over every section, writing down and responding to each question you find relevant. For support, this is best done in a group. Your final assignment is a personal destiny plan, starting with your next step.

Of course, you can just simply read the book and see what sticks! It all depends on what you expect to gain from *More Than Money.* The biggest benefit is seeking and finding your "right place."

More specifically, the book encourages you to *think differently* about career possibilities. MBAs have broader opportunities than most people in their career choices but often feel their options are limited. *More Than Money* gives you a more expansive yet more personal perspective on career decisions and the opportunity to explore your deepest desires. It supports you to follow your dreams and make a contribution.

Getting on your destiny path *sooner* is a second benefit. Too often people fail to make necessary changes until the pain of not changing becomes greater than the fear of change. *More Than Money* should reduce your fear of change and thus the time you spend not living your life. Through the perspective of your destiny path, the book reframes your perceived risks and the rewards expected from various career choices. You'll also have more time to build a community to support you through life's ups and downs.

The third benefit is for you to *feel happier and more fulfilled*. More *Than Money* can help you unlock your passion and be true to yourself. If you do, compassion will follow. There's a symbiotic relationship between serving yourself and serving others. You can even be a "hard-core" MBA but still benefit from finding or creating work that is closer to the values of your heart. And in so doing, you'll inevitably end up giving more to others.

More *Than Money* offers a unique continuum from self-actualization (Chapters 1 and 2) to a service-based life (Chapters 3 and 4). It's up to you how far you want to go. Clarifying your values and trying to create or find work that expresses those values may be enough for now. Each step in the process of serving yourself and serving others is important for spending your time as you like.

As the *New York Times* reported, every living thing has about one billion heartbeats. *What will you do with your billion?*

Book Overview

More *Than Money* guides you through four essential questions and twelve lifelines that will help you examine your life and find your path of service and fulfillment. I don't expect you to connect with every lifeline or story, but I'm sure you'll find plenty of stories and "sticky" questions embedded in the text to help you construct your destiny plan.

Setting a foundation for the four questions, the Introduction holds a mirror up to your business school experiences. Drawing on hundreds of questions raised at my school sessions and thousands of e-mails I've received over the past two decades, I offer something you've probably never seen before: I paint a picture of your challenges, anxieties, pressures, and options, understanding that no one size fits all. Ideally, this portrait will help you to rethink your risk-reward perceptions and how the MBA environment affects those perceptions.

Chapters 1 through 4 present the four chapter title questions and twelve lifelines. The four questions are (1) "Who are you?"; (2) "What do you want?"; (3) "What can you do?"; and (4) "Where are you going?" It is important to read these chapters in order. Most of you start your life at question 3, "What can you do?" rather than asking more reflective questions of yourself first—"Who are you?" and "What do you want?" Without that knowledge, how can you construct an authentic personal compass for a career path, no less a destiny path?

Each chapter offers three lifelines. These lifelines are intended as guidelines for your life that will keep you from drowning—from getting off course. As I mentioned, the first two chapters (the first six lifelines) are internally focused to help you learn more about yourself. To translate the first six into a destiny path requires that you explore the next six externally focused lifelines, too.

Here's each lifeline with a description:

Chapter 1: Who Are You?

You start by unlocking what you're passionate about.

1. *Don't Get Really Good at What You Don't Want to Do.* You're told you're good at something when you're young, and that's that. Years later, you realize that you're really passionate about something else. At business school, it's pretty much about being good at marketing or finance. But each one of you has special gifts. Have the courage to find them and be the best you—even if it is in marketing or finance!

2. *Listen to the Little Voice.* Adult conditioning and the voices of your family, friends, peers, and society have overwhelmed your childhood instincts. At business school, hallway bulletin boards and digital televisions tell you what that voice should be. Don't forget your instincts, expressed in your unique inner voice. You need to notice and develop that voice for the outside world.

3. *Broaden Your Vision of Life.* You are born into one vision of the world: yours. At business school, you study several different case situations but learn one way of approaching them. It's important to meet and learn from all kinds of people with different perspectives about life to help you round out what you believe in and how you want to touch the world.

Chapter 2: What Do You Want?

You need to know what is important to you and what your priorities are to begin on any path. You will get a four-part tool to measure what you want.

4. *Know How You Measure Success.* Only you can define what constitutes personal success. It may have many dimensions and change over time. At business school, the measurement of success is often assumed. It's up to you to proactively search for your definition and use it as your North Star.

5. *Money Doesn't Talk, It Swears.* I assume that one of your goals is making a good living. This lifeline serves to reemphasize how important money is in most lives. How you make it, what you do with it, and how much of it you consider is "enough" are tests of your character. At business school, its primacy is assumed. Getting your attitude toward money straight is crucial to future career opportunities and personal happiness.

6. *Don't Treasure Your Trash and Trash Your Treasures.* As high achievers, it's easy for MBAs to get sidetracked. In business school, that assumed set of values looms behind every conversation. Make sure you're able to keep your priorities straight when the pressure of the business world conflicts with your values.

Chapter 3: What Can You Do?

The book takes on a cautionary tone to ensure that you find the right place to bring your values to work—today.

7. *Turn Your Values into Value.* Now that you understand who you are and what you want, it's time to apply your passion and values to your work. At business school, elective courses or extracurricular activities can prepare you. But at work, creating value is less about your skills and more about your will to fight for what you believe in. You will go through a four-step process for creating value.

8. *Keep Your Walking Costs Low.* This lifeline is at the heart of reframing your perceptions of risk. At business school, you discuss economic risk and possibly "performance" risk. Yet it is a third kind of risk, psychosocial risk, that can dominate your life and needs to be managed, too.

9. *Don't Live a Deferred Life Plan.* When considering career changes, there are always reasons to delay. Yet after making a change, most MBAs wish they had done so sooner. At business school, the focus is on your first job out of school in a select number of high-paying fields. MBAs today are examining other paths. Make sure you don't forget what you learned in the first six lifelines and delay too long.

Chapter 4: Where Are You Going?

Shifting from approaching your career as a job to regarding it as a vocation, a calling, you focus on the service aspects of your destiny plan and refine it.

10. *Look Not at the Masses but at the One.* In crafting your destiny plan, it is easy to think of "contribution" or "impact" as requiring size and scale. That can be daunting. At business school, you get caught up in the law of growth for impact. But it's easier and often more effective to start small and even to stay that way. Size and scale are not as important as purpose.

11. *Surround Yourself with a Community of Love.* MBAs who are happiest at work often say it is because of their relationships with colleagues and clients. At business school, you primarily practice analytical thinking, not relationship building. Don't underestimate the importance of a community of respect and friendship for personal fulfillment and success.

12. *Plant Trees Under Whose Shade You'll Never Sit.* A critical part of any destiny plan is to have an unreachable ultimate goal. Counter to business school teachings of achievable goals, unreachable goals add meaning to your life and energy to your work as they connect you with something bigger than yourself.

The concluding chapter reemphasizes the centrality of service to the process of crafting a life that is more than money. It summarizes the key arguments with a story of the service ethic in a man I met years ago in Goa, India.

A resource chapter follows. It contains a speech that will make you think deeply about your life and the role of money.

I hope that after you've read this book, you'll do some journaling to help you become more aware of who you are and what you want. As you grow, these definitions will evolve as well. Journaling allows you to disconnect from the external electronic world every once in a while and connect to your inner world. How else will you find the work you love and for which others will love and remember you?

It's time to get started by taking a closer look at yourself and the business school environment.

Destiny Plan Questions

▶ What do you see when you look in the mirror? How would you describe yourself?

▶ How would you like to be remembered after you are gone? What would you like your eulogy to be?

▶ In your lifetime, what will your contribution be?

▶ What does "contribution" or "service" mean to you? What role does this concept play for you in having a "meaningful life"?

■ ■ ■ ■ ■ INTRODUCTION: THE MBA TRAP

Money sometimes costs too much.

Ralph Waldo Emerson, poet

MBAs are focused, driven, thoughtful people who typically choose one of two career paths. The first, the more common, is the one I took. I call it the *conflicted achiever* path, expressed as "I'll make some money now, pay off my debts, build a little nest egg, and then . . . who knows? But business school will give me the skills and cachet I need to change careers, move up, and make more money, after which I'll do what I'm passionate about and contribute to society."

The other path is the *passionate striver* path: "I want to do something meaningful now. I already know the kind of work that I find fulfilling. Business school will give me the skills I need to be more effective in my work and a network to draw on for help along the way so that I can advance faster in my career." Both paths are fine as long as you don't get stuck in the wrong job or see your passion frustrated and fade.

The reality is that most MBAs take jobs in management consulting or investment banking. After all, that's what business school does best: train students to be market or financial analysts. Nothing wrong with that. Just remember that few of you grew up dreaming of selling another strategic plan or making another business deal.

The challenge is to use that job in ways that will help you seek and find your unique contribution—which may very well be in consulting or banking. Those professions have also evolved with your interests in mind, offering MBAs work in nonprofit divisions of the most respected consulting firms as others work in "bottom of the pyramid" microfinance at top-tier investment banking companies.

MBAs want to make a contribution through their work, whether it's in the workplace, the marketplace, or the community. This was not as true in my day, but today it's true of the vast majority. You're different, and the world you're inhabiting is different. Even my venerable school, staid Harvard Business School, changed its mission in the twenty-first century to "educating leaders who make a difference in the world."

What I've seen at the business schools is, as I like to say, "You've got the religion. You just don't know how to get to church." Regardless of which of the two initial career paths you choose—or some combination of the two—the work of this book is to help you get to a place where you're appreciated and can make a contribution to others that's worth more than money.

In that spirit, the book's central argument is that if you put *contribution*— crucial to a meaningful life—on an equal footing with money, *what you perceive as your safest career choices may actually be your riskiest, and vice versa.* That is, if you assess risk with the career goal of a meaningful life (which includes making money), you'll make different choices or at least be more aware of the risk-reward trade-offs of your choices and choose a job that is more likely to be on your destiny path.

Whether you are searching more for money or meaning initially, each path has its negative externalities. However, you often recognize the externalities of choosing more satisfying work but overlook them when you choose the employer who shows you the money.

That's the MBA trap: improperly assessing the risk-reward ratio in your career choices by not including all the externalities. This trap occurs when you measure success just by money rather than including the desire to make a contribution as part of a *meaningful life*. With a meaningful life as your goal instead of money, your definitions of *safe* and *risky* change: you now recognize that a "safe" job choice is one that you believe is on your destiny path, and a "risky" choice is one that is not.

To explain, I'd like to share a parable that resonates with MBAs more than any other story I know. I believe it gets you to reconsider what constitutes a successful life.

The Good Life: A Parable

The career perspective of the MBA environment may be best expressed in a parable you won't find in business school. It has received the most responses from MBAs in all my years of writing. I first published it over a decade ago after returning from an idyllic week on an island of just seventy people. I spent my days diving with local dive master Ollie Bean and imagined what it would be like if he met up with the Harvard Business School student in me.

My purpose is to show how your higher education and the values and expectations that often go with it might lead you away from a life path that is enjoyable, rewarding, and contributory. With minor editing,[1] here's "The Good Life":

An American businessman was at the pier of a small coastal Mexican village when a small boat with a lone fisherman docked. Inside the boat were several large yellowfin tuna. He complimented the fisherman on the quality of fish and asked how long it took to catch them. "Only a little while," the fisherman replied.

The businessman then asked why didn't he stay out longer and catch more fish. The fisherman said he had enough to support his family's needs. The businessman asked, "What do you do with the rest of your time?" The fisherman said, "I sleep late, fish a little, play with my children, take siesta with my wife, Maria, and then teach children how to fish before I stroll into the village each evening where I sip wine and play guitar with my friends. I have a full and busy life."

The businessman laughed at him. "I am an MBA and could help you. You should spend more time fishing and with the proceeds buy a bigger boat. With

---

[1] I've since seen this parable in many forms to which my monthly e-newsletter readers have directed my attention, so it is clear that others have written similar stories. The earliest I have found is *"Anekdote von der Senkung der Arbeitsmoral"* ("Anecdote to Reduce the Work Ethic"), written in 1963 by the German Nobel Prize laureate Heinrich Böll, nearly identical but used differently. A similar tale apparently also appears in a Buddhist story and in Russian folklore.

the proceeds from the bigger boat you could buy several boats. Eventually you would have a fleet of fishing boats. Instead of selling your catch to a middleman you would sell directly to the processor. Eventually you could open your own cannery. You would control the product, processing, and distribution."

"And then what would I do?" the fisherman wondered.

"You would then, of course, need to leave this small coastal fishing village and move to Mexico City, then probably Los Angeles, and eventually locate in New York City, where you would run your expanding enterprise."

The fisherman asked, "How long will this all take?" "Ten to fifteen years," the MBA replied. "But what then, señor?" The MBA laughed, saying that's the best part: "When the time is right, you would announce an IPO [initial public offering] and sell your company stock to the public. You would become very rich, making millions of dollars."

"Millions? Then what?"

The MBA businessman concluded, "Then you would retire. Move to a small coastal fishing village where you would sleep late, fish a little, play with your kids, take siesta with your wife, and then teach children how to fish before you stroll into the village each evening where you could sip wine and play your guitar with your friends."

A simple parable worth reading again, "The Good Life" is about values often taken for granted as the material world and its partner "greed" pull you away from yourself, magnified in most business school settings.

Your Business School Environment

Business schools have a culture that narrows your perceived options and can often direct your behavior as a businessperson, at least early in your career, by the values espoused. What are those values?[2]

In the 1970s, the elite business schools were organized around the goal of producing general managers. The CEO as enlightened corporate statesman

---

[2] The next three paragraphs are based on Rakhesh Khurana, *From Higher Aims to Hired Hands: The Social Transformation of American Business Schools and the Unfulfilled Promise of Management Education* (Princeton, N.J.: Princeton University Press, 2007).

was still of interest, although it would fade in the 1980s with the emergence of investor capitalism and its takeover wave.

By 1980, business experts wrote that countries like Japan were turning out better managers. American managers needed to learn how to manage more effectively toward one goal: maximization of corporate value. Shareholder primacy became the new mantra. The *New York Times* duly noted that the new model of corporate "goodness . . . eschews loyalty to workers, products, corporate structures, businesses, factories, communities, even the nation." The new flood of corporate takeovers meant that only "maximizing stock price can be allowed to matter." This maxim would dominate the culture of most business schools.

These arguments led to aligning managers' incentives with those of shareholders. The executive option market flourished, one of the most disastrous developments in the history capitalism. It exacerbated the fixation on short-term profit regardless of longer-term cost. The same ethos would dominate the culture of business schools.

The era can be summed up by an early-1990s televised comment by a large insurance company CEO who resigned soon after the interview. He had agreed to come on the show to discuss the company's new innovative employee assistance programs for minimum-wage workers. But the interviewer focused on the just released quarterly results, which were one penny below expectations. The CEO's comment: "Now I get it. If you want to do something that serves the interests of society, the environment, the community, or the poor, and it *costs your shareholders one penny*, it is immoral."

In October 1993, Net Impact (known until 1999 as Students for Responsible Business) was created to build a community of MBAs that believed that the responsibility of a corporation is not just to shareholders but to all stakeholders. Managing Director Daniel O'Connor best expressed Net Impact's business philosophy in a 1999 speech at the University of Michigan. Daniel explained that the purpose of business is to create value for its society. Through a mission-driven network of emerging business leaders united by a shared commitment to use the power of their *careers*, Net Impact would create a better world for all.

In the 1990s, the majority of business schools saw Net Impact as a fringe group primarily consisting of liberal "tree-huggers" and "do-gooders." But as the twenty-first century dawned, the new global economy transformed the cost-benefit parameters of business through the market realities of climate change, the price of oil, and the demand for young talent who often have social and environmental interests. Net Impact began to grow rapidly as a network for emerging progressive business leaders.

As I write, Net Impact has over 190 business school and professional chapters and is growing rapidly worldwide, with its first European office and chapters in Asia, Africa, and Latin America. At many business schools, Net Impact is the largest student group. Net Impact and its local chapters have also been instrumental in changing business school curriculum while unleashing an energy best seen at the annual conference, which hosts two thousand attendees.

This decade has seen the rising prominence of Aspen Institute's Beyond Grey Pinstripes school rankings. The biennial rankings are based on how well business schools integrate social and environmental stewardship into their curriculum and research. Students are demanding that curriculum more closely reflect their values, and business schools are accommodating those changes. Green business courses were available at nearly two-thirds of business schools surveyed in 2007, twice as many as in 2001.

Still, how much have the schools themselves *really* changed? Schools have opened institutes, some jointly with other university departments, and many offer elective courses in sustainable business, microfinance, corporate social responsibility, and social enterprise. Yet there remain no tenured or tenure-track professors in these fields, indicating that the values espoused by these courses are still not central to most business schools.

Business schools remain driven by rankings and fundraising (helped by higher rankings). Rankings are determined in part by the starting salaries of graduates, not whether they like their jobs or can express their values at work. Where can MBA graduates get the highest starting salaries? See your options narrowing?

For the most part, the bottom line remains the same. As reported in "A Growth Industry" in the April 14, 2008, issue of *Newsweek*, business schools are adopting the philosophy "make a bunch of green by going green"; indeed, the article's subtitle states, "business schools are teaching entrepreneurs how to get rich helping to save the environment."

Interest in a "triple bottom line" can be accommodated as long as the financial bottom line is satisfied. Like Wal-Mart and Toyota, two companies invested in "greening" their companies, environmental responsibility is a *business* calculation of innovative ways to save and make money.

One student at Aspen's top-ranked school, Stanford University, said it best. A twenty-nine-year old with an engineering background, he spent two years studying environmentally sustainable business. Is he doing this because of his values? "The honest answer is no. It makes good business sense to be sustainable." He hopes to be working at a private-equity fund upon graduation.

Whether curriculum change leads to cultural change remains to be seen. Business schools reflect the interests of the surrounding business community, particularly their alums. As green business opportunities in clean technology have grown, curricula have grown in these areas, too. There are now a handful of new schools like Presidio School of Management and Bainbridge Graduate Institute, where sustainable business practices are not a calculation but a *commitment* to social justice and environmental responsibility as much as financial results.

To conclude, business school remains focused on your financial growth, not personal growth. I believe you get *at best* only marginal help in business school at understanding your values and what is important to *you* in your career.

If you don't know exactly what you want to get out of business school, then the business school's curriculum and culture will do little to help you clarify your purpose, awaken your passion, and realize your potential. Just look at the pressures and challenges the typical MBA faces.

A Mirror on MBA Decision Making

With the pressure of job interviews starting in early September (in my day, none were allowed until March), the driving determinant for most students remains money. You take time from work and pay tuition for which you expect a good return, a hefty ROI (return on investment).

Much has changed during my thirty-five years with MBAs, but career decision making has not changed measurably. Synthesizing what you've told me over the past five years in conversations and e-mails, your decisions are primarily driven by six factors:

- ► MBAs often don't consider their own values very high on the list of motivations in making a career decision.

- ► MBAs are not usually encouraged to consult a personal compass to direct their goals when making career decisions.

- ► MBAs feel peer pressure to earn a lot of money when they enter the working world after graduation.

- ► MBAs are expected to measure success in money and public recognition rather than in personal fulfillment.

- ► MBAs are risk-averse, so they often choose to make career decisions that they're supposed to make rather than the decisions their hearts would have them make.

- ► MBAs fear that taking a job that fulfills their heart's desires will not provide enough money to live on.

You may not see yourself in this description of the "typical" MBA. Good for you! But most business schools reinforce this stereotype. To remain atypical, you need to be clear about your answers to the four chapter questions and stick to them. The questions and lifelines can help reaffirm your thinking and existing career goals and aspirations and turn them into a plan of action for your future, your personal destiny plan.

Let me illustrate these six factors in three pairs with examples to help deepen your understanding of how this kind of decision making can limit your options and pull you away from your destiny path.

- ► MBAs often don't consider their own values very high on the list of motivations in making a career decision and are not usually encouraged to consult a personal compass to direct their goals when making career decisions.

MBA graduates have often told me that one of the most important determinants of their happiness and career success has been making the right choice of where they want to live and then looking at job possibilities. Finding the right place to live and work, however, is often considered a low priority in the business school environment.

Recruiters see most MBAs heading to corporate America, working as long as they can stand it, and then striking out for the "small time." Small time? Why not start there? Why not stay with the good life, like the Mexican fisherman? Why not focus on achieving a life of working and living in a place you belong, doing work that matters with people you care about?

Instead, many MBAs may be destined to be ruled by the "Paul Principle." Akin to the Peter Principle ("You are promoted until you reach a job at which you are incompetent"), it states, "You are promoted until your job is no longer fun." Feel free to substitute *career* or *life* for *job*. And you can substitute *moved* (geographically) for *promoted*.

I take the recruiters' insight personally. After just my first term teaching at Harvard Business School, I knew I was in the wrong place. I was not on my path and felt I had to leave my values at home. (It took me six more years to leave.) I was stunned. After all, I'd dreamed of a job like this. My income shot up well into the six figures; my time was my own; I had no direct boss and was surrounded by brilliant, diligent colleagues and students. The Harvard name opened every door imaginable, and the senior faculty could not have treated me better.

I found it hard to get out of bed each day and make it to school, but I persevered. I figured there was something wrong with me. And the results were obvious. My teaching was average at best, and my research stumbled along, though I received more credit than I deserved. I was blessed with the "appearance" of a Harvard Business School professor, the "carriage" of those times. I was afforded every advantage possible—to no avail.

I needed permission to reframe my thinking about what is important in life and how to measure success. I needed to use my personal compass. Instead, I had taken what I considered to be the safest path, the one with the most money and status, and yet I almost lost myself in it. Being a Harvard professor was a great job that offered me a great career. But it wasn't the right one *for me*. I would eventually be supported by business students I met through Net Impact to rethink my career and the role of business.

> ▶ MBAs feel peer pressure to earn a lot of money when they enter the working world after graduation and are expected to measure success in money and public recognition rather than in personal fulfillment.

Most of you will feel that peer pressure to achieve a certain level of "success," which includes a high salary but not necessarily happiness and fulfillment. And the business world reinforces it. For example, during her job search, Maureen Gilbert, a twenty-six-year old INSEAD MBA, wrote me about the "soul price" of financially remunerative work you don't really like:

The more in touch your job is with your soul, the less your wage matters to you. Talk to anyone that isn't happy with his or her job or that secretly dreams of doing something else and nine times out of ten, money will be the reason why they don't leave. So, what is your soul price? *How much do you need to be paid to do a job you really don't love?* [her italics].

Maybe you think you won't make it without a "safety net." Maybe you feel the timing isn't right. It's always more comfortable to go the "safe" route. But what if you never get on that other route?

You know that life is about more than making money and spending it. But on a practical daily basis, you can forget too easily, especially in business school. The result is that you make your alma mater (and possibly parents) happy by selling your soul to the highest bidder. There's a price to be paid, however; a price perhaps unrecognized at first, to be paid years later. As the years increase, so does the soul price. Why do you sell your soul so easily, so cheaply, to the highest bidder without knowledge of the price?

> ▶ MBAs are risk-averse, so they often choose to make career decisions that they're supposed to make rather than the decisions their hearts would have them make. MBAs fear that taking a job that fulfills their heart's desires will not provide enough money to live on.

When I left Harvard to help MBAs find their path of service, I was concerned about my drop in income. I did well enough for years, but the last few years, my pro bono work has been out of balance.

When I was speaking to MBAs at Portland State in 2006, I heard a question that has yet to leave me. It was in response to a student's statement about the need to make money first and then find fulfillment—if for no other reason than to pay off school loans. Work that was closer to his heart would clearly be sacrificed. Another student responded by asking him and the audience, "How far are you from the gutter?"

Think about that. You have many ways to get by: friends and family who will help you and work you could do if necessary. You need to let go of that excuse for not taking the road less traveled—*your* road, the road that's made to fit one person at a time.

Your Safest Choices May Be Your Riskiest

To repeat my definition of *safe* and *risky* career choices:

A *"safe"* job choice is one that you believe is on your destiny path.

A *"risky"* choice is one that is not.

I don't know whether your "safe" choice will be a high-paying, high-prestige job, an entrepreneurial launch, or the distribution of relief services in Darfur. I know that what you need to do to stay on your path will vary over the course of your life. And I know that whatever it is, it will be meaningful to you and of service to others. Is money important? Of course it is, in balance with contribution to others.

What are the "riskiest" choices? Those that don't allow you to become the person you want to be, to live your life full measure. Survey results of the general population confirm that people's biggest fear is neither death (which ranks third) nor public speaking (second) but "failing to live a meaningful life." That's our greatest fear, our biggest risk. And it all begins with not living *your* life.

I fear not living my life. I fear looking in the mirror and not liking what I see. I fear not having the right regrets. I fear not being the best me, of dying with my music still inside. Whenever I ask myself, "If I do this, what's the worst that could happen?" it's rarely worse than not living my life out loud.

I realize that in the business school environment, these are not the standard definitions of safety and risk. I realize that you are given a narrow range of career options to choose from, unless you want to search outside the traditional recruiting opportunities. And I realize the challenge of being highly risk-averse with all the pressure and expectations of what you will do with that great opportunity of an MBA. You're also very good at putting pressure on yourself.

I was concerned about how I'd honor all the sacrifices my parents had made to get me through school. But as a parent, I now realize that whereas I might not understand my children at first, what I most want is for them to be happy and contribute to society. I also want them to reframe the voices of judgment they will hear that may pull them away from their destiny path.

The next four chapters will help you reframe and redefine your notion of the risk-reward trade-off in a way that works for you. It's a way you always knew but have forgotten. Once there, you'll see that the riskiest outcomes for the head are often the least risky for the heart. What seemed like the safest choice in your current environment may preclude happiness and fulfillment down the road. Or at least, slow you down a bit.

One statistic stunned me into rethinking my career, how I spent my time, and how I did or did not live my values. I learned several years ago that the country of Tanzania, with its twenty-five million people, had a gross domestic product that year less than what a well-known investment bank made and shared among its 161 partners. Now, don't go rushing to that investment bank for a job just yet! That wasn't my point. My point is, aren't these truths today that should not be truths tomorrow?

I know that in the time it took you to read the preceding paragraph (twenty seconds), one hundred children died of starvation. I know that over four billion people don't have enough to eat. I don't let these facts paralyze me, nor am I going off to live like Mother Teresa. But I do know that those realities make me think more deeply about what I can do to make a difference through the most powerful force on the planet (no, it's not compound interest): business.

A decade ago, I was asked in front of four hundred University of Michigan alums to describe in one sentence what is a good business. I was caught off guard and had little time to think. Normally, my response would have been about serving all the stakeholders. Instead, what came out of me was this: "A good business uplifts the human spirit and helps alleviate poverty and suffering on the planet."

After I said it, you could have heard a pin drop in the room! I heard mumblings like, "Are we at the Divinity School or the Business School?" For the next ninety minutes, however, the questions all had a different tone. That evening, we looked at the business world and our careers from the perspective of my definition. I've since used that expression as my personal North Star. You'll find your star by working through Chapters 1 and 2 and then applying what you learn there in Chapters 3 and 4.

Destiny Plan Questions

▶ Which career path is more in line with your thinking: (1) make some money first and then focus more on what you are passionate about, or (2) focus on what you are passionate about right away? What are the risks and rewards of each?

▶ What do you see as a "safe" job choice and as a "risky" job choice? Why?

▶ What do or did you expect to get out of business school? Did the school experience meet your expectations?

▶ What is the purpose of business?

CHAPTER 1 ■ ■ ■ ■ ■ WHO ARE YOU?

If the things we believe are different than the things we do, there can be no true happiness.

David O. McKay
Ninth president of the Mormon Church

It was that day in 1943. A nineteen-year-old boy from Dorchester, Massachusetts, had become a low-beam radar navigator in the Eighth Division of the United States Air Force. And today was the day that he would fly his first mission—over Germany. That day, this boy had to make a decision that would leave childhood far behind: whether or not to wear the Jewish Star of David on his missions. He knew the price he might pay if his plane were shot down. He knew his chances of survival would plummet if he were caught wearing that Star.

He decided to wear that Star. When he did, he joined peoples from all nations, religions, races, and creeds who have chosen throughout the course of human history to uphold their beliefs and heritage in the face of persecution, torture, and even death. As that legendary Scot, William Wallace of *Braveheart* fame, exhorted his men, "Cowards die many times; brave men die only once."

By declaring himself publicly, my father told the world and himself who he was, who he wanted to be, and what he believed in. By that one act, he took the abstract concepts of values, conscience, and personal responsibility and made them real, creating a living heritage for his future family.

I often think of my father's challenge. I ask, "What is *my* Star of David? What are the values that direct my decisions? What am I passionate about, whatever the cost?"

My father was not a zealot or even a practicing Jew. He chose to wear that Star of David because it was how he made sense of his world and his place in it. Although he wasn't aware of it then, in many ways that singular decision would define his life forever. It helped him come to terms with who he was. It was also the greatest gift he took into civilian life. That reckoning imprinted by thirty-five missions gave him the confidence to develop a winning career after the war. He found himself and his internal compass through his allegiance to that Star.

I'm sometimes jealous of my father's "opportunity" to discover who he was and what he stood for. Whereas his life was put at risk, the war forced him to dig deep into his soul and clarify his passion to be a Jew and an inner drive to win, whatever the odds.

Few of you will experience such a dramatic situation. Yet to realize your potential by fulfilling your destiny, you too need to search inside yourself to awaken what makes you come alive with passion and without fear. This chapter guides you with the first step in creating your destiny plan: three lifelines that open your heart and your inner self. By working through the twelve lifelines and addressing the questions offered that most resonate with you, you will have written down the basic information you need to construct your destiny plan. Think of it as your personal, *authentic* strategic plan.

I think it might be helpful for you to see a brief description of my destiny plan to guide you in developing your own. Without a timetable or more specifics, the plan that serves as my North Star appears at the top of the next page. As you can see, a destiny plan is not a résumé, nor is it a description of any particular job. It is a summary of your hopes and dreams and how you will make a contribution to a better world. Like the word *service*, it is less about a specific act

Goal:	*To help MBAs find their path of service*
Why:	*To* humanize *the way we do business in the world and to make sure no MBA has to give up making a life to make a living*
How:	*Through work I enjoy, including writing, speaking, and advising*
Values:	*The highest integrity and personal freedom*

than an attitude, a *consciousness* of how you want to affect people and the planet, all living things. It is not only a window into the future but also a mirror to let you look at yourself today.

Constructing a destiny plan therefore requires you to address all four chapter title questions and a significant number of the other sixty-four "destiny plan" questions in the book. Select the questions that you find most helpful in reframing your risk-reward assessment of different job alternatives. Chapters 1 and 2 will offer a mirror in six lifelines to help you understand yourself. In my description, my responses are recorded in the "how" and "values" lines. Self-actualization, learning how to serve yourself, is a big step for most of you, something you are not taught in school.

Chapters 3 and 4 offer guidance for the next step: bringing your dreams and desires into the marketplace of your life (the "goal" and "why" responses to the challenges of this chapter and the next). These chapters do not tell you what to do or what job to pick. They are more cautionary in tone. Their purpose is not to carve out your path for you but rather to give you the greatest opportunity to find your path, stay on it, and get back on it more quickly when you fall off.

Today, your career, your destiny, is in your hands. Your destiny is something you *achieve*. With your passion and values as your guides, your ultimate success will be less a function of your abilities and more the result of your choices— choices of "small deeds done with great love," in Mother Teresa's words.

First Steps: Unlocking the Courage to Be Yourself

In your career search, how you begin affects where you'll end up. It's much easier to make small adjustments than to reroute your entire path (though it can be done). Your foundation and starting point are based on discovering who you are and what you want—your value and values that come from deep inside. You need to fight being defined by what you do and first and foremost discover who you are, what you stand for, and what you believe in. Otherwise you risk being stuck in a career you never really wanted.

Your guide is your passion. It's what makes you special. I'm surprised by how many MBAs write me that there's nothing special about them. In Leviticus 19:2, God says, "You shall be holy because I the Lord Your God am holy." For me, saying we are "holy" is another way of saying that we each are special beings with a special purpose and that we reach that purpose through study, prayer, and deeds of loving-kindness. Whether you are a Bible reader or not, that's still a powerful way to start off thinking about your career!

Your passion will allow you to get lost in something bigger than yourself, as it is that passion—your *will*, not your skills—that will define you and make you great. That's how you *find* yourself: by getting *lost* in something you feel has importance beyond yourself. It may be addressing a social challenge, building a company, or collaborating with colleagues to meet a deadline. And when you can meet a business need *and* a social need, especially if it is *personal*, the feeling is priceless. As an example, look no further than social entrepreneur Joe Sibilia.

Joe houses a series of businesses called Gasoline Alley in a troubled area of his blue-collar hometown, Springfield, Massachusetts. Buildings and furniture are constructed from discarded materials and recycled products, and the 375 feet of front footage and acres behind have been renovated organically. Prisoners and former drug addicts, people "discarded by society," populate the businesses. What is Joe doing? "You ask me what the mission of my business is? It's to give value to that which has been abandoned."

Compassion comes from being linked to your passion. Joe's dedication to the "abandoned," to a neighborhood that he could have left decades ago when his financial success first began, is personal. It comes from his past. "When I was born, my folks split up, Dad moved out, and soon thereafter Mom left. My brother is ten years older, and he left, too. An aunt came to live with me. My real support came from the 'guys on the Corner.'"

The Corner is where Joe hung out, growing up in Springfield with few resources but big dreams. His buddies went through a life of difficulties. Today many of them work for Joe at Gasoline Alley, finding new life and purpose.

Joe has owned over twenty companies; you too will have many changes in your work. But whereas the form of what you do may change, that core of who you are, often developed in your early adolescent years, doesn't change. It gets tested and grows.

Finding out who you are and where you belong is often a process of finding out where you fit in by not fitting in. It's a lonely business, trying to fit in and failing. But that's what you have to do. It typically starts when you're a child, around nine to twelve years old.

What Did You Want to Do Before the World "Should" on You?

This is another way of asking yourself to try to remember your childhood instincts and aspirations before adult conditioning took over. You may have considered that lemonade stand "play" back then, but in many ways, you were experimenting in a child's version of making a living. For me, it took my younger daughter's impression of who I was, sharpened by her instincts of what I enjoyed, to get me back on track in my mid-forties.

When my daughter Nicolette (Nikki) was five (she's now seventeen), she drew a picture of who she thought her Daddy was and what he loves to do—two ideas linked inextricably as one for her. Her drawing, along with her description of me appears on the next page.

She was right. Earlier that year, I'd gone up into my attic and found the proverbial "box in the attic" of memories buried, suppressed, and repressed long ago. In a box were short stories I had completely forgotten about! I now remembered what served as my "lemonade stand."

"My Dad has a big head and a big mouth, with a stubby little body. [*That's OK—she gave me a lot of hair!*] Here he is next to his 'puter. What my Dad loves to do is type. He loves to type."

When I was eight years old, I'd write these stories, type them up, and get them mimeographed at my grandfather's office. I'd then sell them door-to-door: 3 cents for a one-page story, 5 cents for a two-page story. The stories had titles like "I Went Mad," "I Was the Fiery Demon," and "Friday the 13th." (What do you want? I was just a kid and obviously no Hemingway.) As you might expect, no one in the neighborhood turned me down. And it certainly beat having a paper route. But what was the message I got at home? "You can't be a writer. Writers don't make much money." So the dream went into the box.

The next year, I had a counseling business: I would advise my friends on how to get along better with their siblings. (Of course, I myself had no siblings at the time.) I charged a nickel for that service. Like Lucy in the *Peanuts* comic strip, I did well with my little advice stand business. And what was the message I got this time? "That's great, Mark. You want to be a psychiatrist!"

When I explained that I had no intention of becoming a doctor, well, my parents' expressions were ... priceless? I then followed the "I want to be a" with two words that can kill any parents: "social worker." Better to be a sculptor—at least the folks get to see something tangible!

Today, I'm living my childhood dreams. I write and advise. I guess you never truly leave childhood; rather you take a little bit of it with you. For me, it took a daughter's drawing and forty years to get back there! Want to do it sooner? Listen to your children and friends. Think back. What did you want to do in your early days? What lights you up, makes you jump out of bed in the morning, excited by a new day?

It's the complex, wondrous journey of the heart whose only risk is not being true to itself. That's a risk overcome by following the first three lifelines.

Destiny Plan Questions

► What are you passionate about?

► Describe your perfect day. What does your description tell you?

► What did you love to do when you were around eleven or twelve?

► Do you do things that are at odds with what you believe in? If so, what are they, and why do you do them?

Don't Get Really Good
at What You Don't Want to Do

I'm a fan of the comedian Drew Carey, who responds when someone complains about work, "Oh, you hate your job. Why didn't you say so? There's a support group for that. It's called 'Everybody,' and they meet at the bar."

Funny, but sadly true, even among highly educated MBAs—surprising for a community with lucky lottery tickets. You have options but lots of pressures; you fear being an *outsider*—the required identity to follow your own path. You forget that each person has a unique story to live, one that you need to identify and actualize. You forget that work can give you *joy*.

It's easy to slide into a career that matches your skills but not your deepest desires. At first, it can be harder not to do what you are really good at and instead to work at what you really love. And what do you love? Sometimes you're not sure; other times it requires you to balance a cluster of core values that include work, social contribution, family, and personal life (see Lifeline 6 in Chapter 2).

When you get good at something you don't want to do, you feel as if you're dying a little bit each day—that your soul is being sucked out of you. Worse yet, it takes time to realize what's going on. Maybe you don't enjoy your work as much as you used to, or you aren't performing as well as you know you can. Maybe Sunday nights are a misery, causing you to wake with a knot in your stomach Monday morning. Maybe you're wondering, "How did I get here?" That's why I agree with the late George Burns: I'd rather be a failure at something I love than a success at something I hate.

I call "Don't Get Good . . ." my "bobble head" lifeline. When I use this expression in a speech, I can see the heads of my audience bob up and down in acknowledgment. We've all been there. I was a Greek major in college and then wanted to do graduate work in psychology. But I was good at math and economics, so that's where I went. It took me thirty years to get back to Greek (Bible study group) and psychology (my work with MBAs).

I have scores of letters from MBAs talking about jobs they hate but "can't leave" or "don't know how to leave." Here's a sample: "Since I was 15 I wanted to be a teacher and a coach. Instead, after getting my MBA I've chased the golden handcuffs as a management consultant, had IPO dreams with an Internet company, and then ran a hedge fund. I always promised that I wouldn't 'sell out' like so many of my friends who are lawyers or I-bankers. As I sit here watching five computer screens 80 hours a week, I ask myself, What am I building?"

This first lifeline asks you to start your destiny plan, to consider what your contribution will be and your eulogy will say, by clarifying what you don't want to do and who you don't want to be. Start by asking yourself instead, "Who are my heroes, and why do I admire them?" Your answers allow you to visualize your future self so that you can work your way back to what you need to do today—and may not be doing.

My heroes built a strong platform and then used their money and status to have a positive impact on their community and the world. They are Muhammad Ali, Arthur Ashe, Shirley Temple Black, Robert Redford, and Oprah Winfrey. (I also admire my mother and how she has run her business for forty years, as well as several Net Impact MBAs who show me repeatedly what's possible.) Each of these five people will be remembered as athletes or entertainers who gave much of their life energy to serving others. When they pass on, Redford may be more remembered for Sundance and Oprah for her work in Africa then for their "careers."

I have surveyed several thousand MBAs at my speeches. The common "hero" responses include parents and teachers, along with Mother Teresa, Dr. Martin Luther King Jr., Bill Gates, and heads of state who have made a significant contribution to world peace. So ask yourself, "If this is a person I admire, am I on a path to honor what he or she stands for? If not, what changes do I need to make?"

It all comes back to knowing who you are and what your values are. *If you're not clear in defining yourself, others will do it for you.* Moreover, you can become a creature of your uniform. You go from being defined by parents to falling under the influence of your peers, your workplace, and its culture. You become the person of that job. You may be further influenced by well-meaning senior colleagues and lose yourself if you're not careful. I almost did.

I was young when I became a marketing professor at Harvard Business School. I was told that I looked young, too, which only made matters worse. The challenge was that our MBA students are known for their combativeness. They test professors and respect only toughness. Any chink in the armor and "those eighty-eight students of yours will eat you for lunch, Mark." There's nothing worse than losing control of your class. Makes for a long semester.

I listened to all my senior professors' advice. "Have them call you 'Professor Albion,'" "Don't fraternize with students," "If you make a mistake during class, don't admit it," and so on. I even followed their methods of teaching, putting my own style and ideas in a box. After all, what did I know? I knew one thing better than my learned, and concerned, senior professors knew: *Mark Albion.* But I did not stand up for myself or speak with my own voice.

Instead of being called "Mark," which I much prefer, instead of playing touch football with my students (many of whom were my age or older), and instead of admitting calculation errors in class, I didn't, didn't, didn't. When I would speak or ask questions, it was as if I were following someone else's script rather than choosing what I felt was helpful from the mounds of advice and then practicing how I'd like to teach. How I'd like to be.

For a time, I got good at being someone else. But it was a disaster. *I* was a disaster. And I was miserable, too. The least I could have done was fail gloriously! What I had risked was not just what I was doing but *who I was becoming.* I wanted to be a success, to feel success, but how can you when there is no joy? What I needed to do was find my own voice, the second step of a destiny plan.

Destiny Plan Questions

► Who are your heroes? Why?

► Do you dislike what you do? If so, why do you do it?

► Outside your family, what do you do that gives you joy?

Listen to the Little Voice

In the Hebrew Bible it is called your *kol katan,* that little voice inside you, hard to hear but essential to find and use if you are going to fulfill your potential. That voice will connect you with your deep desires and your vocation (from the Latin *vocare,* which means "to call")—*your calling.* That voice will help you touch the world and serve others by drawing on what is deep inside you. That voice is your *authenticity. More Than Money* comes from my little voice.

It takes time, patience, and courage to listen and respond to that little voice. For me, it wasn't until the last two years at Harvard that I began to hear that voice and use it. In the classroom, thirty-five-year-old Mark played his childhood accordion (I have pictures to prove it!). I made calculation mistakes and laughed at myself. I spoke of personal issues and brought my background, my *self,* into the discussion. It was fun, and for the first time, I experienced a classroom of human beings, not just students.

What helped me do it? Partly the pain of not being myself became greater than my fear of being different from what I was told I should be. But what really happened was that I had promised myself and my wife in 1986, when my mother was diagnosed with stage-four cancer, that after she recovered, I would move on to another job. I was no longer worried about pleasing others and getting promoted. As I brought all of me to work, I felt "free" and flourished.

It's hard to feel confident in your abilities and intuition and not mimic others. Cultural dictates are powerful. Those voices of judgment (VOJs, as they're called) can make it difficult to find your voice, to be *you* and not *them.* If you're driven to prove your worthiness to others, you've handed over your life to the VOJs.

At times, you feel like an impostor—a little kid dressed up in big kid's clothing—with a job beyond your abilities. You feel that someone is going to find out and call you to task. Rather than relaxing and being yourself, you get into trouble trying to do stuff that doesn't fit who you are. Finding and sticking with your little voice helps you set your values and focus on what you really want to give and get out of life.

How hard is it? Think of the startling revelation by Senator Hillary Clinton after her surprise win in the New Hampshire presidential primary in January 2008. Following an unusually emotional week of campaigning, she was considered out of the race. She began her victory speech with "I listened to you and in the process found my own voice."

Are you in touch with your little voice? How do you know? One way is to take a look at your body language when you respond to questions about your work in social situations.

For example, I was in New York in 2000 with my leadership consultant, Mike Barr, talking about launching a new executive program. It would be a big money-maker for us both. Mike had four children bound for college in the next few years, so I was sure he would be excited about it. Mike's response: "You went through it beautifully, like a true MBA." He then asked me how my writing was going.

As he told me fifteen minutes later, I nearly "exploded" (his word) in my seat, arms waving wildly as I talked, enthusiasm oozing with every word. He could hardly get in a word himself. He simply smiled. When I finished, I knew what I'd forgotten. My body language had made me aware of my little voice.

When you're in touch with your little voice, you come alive—you are being *you*, being *authentic*. So how do you get in touch with your little voice and bring it into your life? Just answer the question "When do I feel authentic?" Those times are windows to your inner world.

It would take me ten years after playing the accordion in class to give my first speech with my own voice. As you can see from my 2000 conversation with Mike, it's easy to slip back into old habits without friendly advice. As you read through the circumstances of my speech, think about what elements of my story may help you hear your inner voice.

Through chance events, I had the opportunity to give an official speech to the United Nations and its delegates on June 5, 1996. I had done a survey of MBAs' attitudes and values to help promote Net Impact. To get MBA students to fill out an online thirty-five-minute survey, I promised that if a thousand students filled it out, I'd deliver the findings to the United Nations. I had no idea how to get a UN speech, but the "Let Your Voice Be Heard" MBA campaign pulled in twenty-three hundred completed surveys.

Fortunately, through Social Venture Network (SVN) Europe, an Italian colleague arranged two sessions for me at the UN's official conference in Istanbul, Turkey. One was a seminar and the other was a speech to business leaders. I delivered the findings to the three hundred business leaders and got ready to go home after a day of relaxation with SVN friends.

The official speeches to the delegates began two days later. A top U.S. educator was to deliver a speech on the role of education in creating socially responsible, young global business leaders. Unfortunately, her brother was killed back in the States, and she had to rush home. A replacement was needed, an educator. Though I balked, my friends made it clear that this was something that I had to do.

I spent the next two days practicing a twelve-minute speech that I was given to read verbatim to the assembly of delegates and guests. It was handed to UN translators, too. It was technically an excellent speech, but it had no heart, no soul. How could I give such a dry, uninspiring speech about educating the next generation to help the homeless and the needy of the world?

Before the session, I promised myself two things: that I would not be nervous so I could enjoy the two-and-a-half-hour session (five twelve-minute speeches and discussion time) and that I'd give the speech from my heart.

I was the third speaker. As the second presenter wound down, I could see the delegates nodding off. Listening to a speech read word for word is not exciting. About five minutes before my turn, I decided not to use the prepared speech and just speak from my heart, without notes. (This was a little hard on the translators, but they caught up quickly.)

To my surprise, I gave the speech of my life. I talked about lessons on compassion from my daughters and the importance of service work in developing responsible young leaders. I discussed the heart of the survey results and the importance of a career that addresses social challenges. As I gave the speech, I felt bathed in a light of peace and comfort. No nerves. Tranquillity. Whatever I said, while I knew it wouldn't be perfect, I also knew it would be from the heart. It would have energy behind it. *It would be me.* And the delegates could tell.

When I finished, I felt as if a great weight had been lifted from my shoulders. For once, I didn't need any compliments, though the next day I'd meet a member of the audience, whose complimentary words still mean a great deal to me. I would have never met her if I hadn't listened to and spoken with my voice.

What does this "little voice" look like? Mother Teresa expressed hers on the calling card she'd hand to people. It read:

> *The fruit of SILENCE is Prayer*
> *The fruit of PRAYER is Faith*
> *The fruit of FAITH is Love*
> *The fruit of LOVE is Service*
> *The fruit of SERVICE is Peace*

How better to describe the essence of Mother Teresa? That little voice allows you to close the chasm between the divine and the human, between doctrine and doing.

What can you take from my story? When I look back, I realize that by following the love—my passion for Net Impact—and serving like-minded people whose concerns are my concerns (SVN), if I take a deep breath and trust in those people who care about me, they will help me dig deeper and be true to that little voice. It means taking risks (the trip had many complications) and letting go of control at times. It requires you to not think too much.

Listening to your *inner* voice requires you to go *outside* yourself and be aware of what's happening around you. Rarely do these life experiences come from "straight ahead." More often than not, they occur when you least expect them, when you are doing things you don't normally do. Maybe it's when you are doing a special favor or attending a particular function for the first time. They come "out of nowhere." But nowhere is somewhere when you broaden your vision.

Destiny Plan Questions

► When do you feel authentic?

► Who are your voices of judgment? What do they say, and how do you deal with them?

► If you had a calling card, like Mother Teresa, what would yours say?

■ **LIFELINE 3** ■

Broaden Your Vision of Life

Management consultant Peter Patch described to my MBA class what he learned at business school. A Stanford MBA, Peter responded that as business school is primarily an education in how to develop your own way of making decisions, whenever he had to make a decision, he'd call a dozen of his brightest friends and get their take, to make sure he hadn't overlooked something. "Perspective is worth 100 IQ points," he summarized.

Two decades later, on September 11, 2006, I was near Ground Zero. After my speech to nonprofit executives, I was asked what is the most important quality for young leaders. I responded that it was *multicultural sensitivity*. Who you are as a leader is defined not only by your own inner sense of being but also by your relationships with others. More than ever before, these relationships are with people from different cultures and ways of life. Understanding them and how to work with them is critical to becoming a successful leader in the twenty-first century.

These two aspects of broadening your vision—perspective and understanding—form what I call my "travel the world and talk to grandmas" lifeline. This lifeline asks you to broaden and deepen your understanding of who you are through a range of relationships so that you don't risk limiting your potential.

That there are different perspectives on ways of living life was the most important lesson I learned from my backpacking trip around the world. In trying to become "me," there wasn't just the one way I had learned in the

Boston-Washington corridor of careers of achievement and contribution. There were many other ways to be a successful human being.

I traveled by bus and third-class train and even hitchhiked, all of which allowed me to meet people I'd never normally meet. And of course, I spent time with the grandmothers, the keepers of the cultures. Years later, I realized how that experience had deepened my knowledge of myself in a way that school or work never could.

At the MBA career restaurant, you're fed a narrow selection of meals to represent the menu of life. What is or is not success is made clear. Anything off the menu is considered high risk. Yet I believe that even though those few options may help you start on the path of who you want to become, there are many others that may suit some of you better. Without investigating those options, you are taking a greater risk: setting out on your path with a shaky foundation.

In some cultures, for example, who *you* are is understood through the lens of who *we* are. In South Africa, the African aphorism "I am because we are" guides personhood. If you want to know a person, you must know the community, for it is the community that makes us who we are. So if you want to meet someone properly, you should learn about the community that raised that person. If you were visiting, say, Nelson Mandela, it would be best to read about Transkei, the region where he was born, and Qunu, the village where he was raised.

That's the paradox of individuality, not just in South Africa but to some extent everywhere. Who we are is very much in relation to others, to a set of values and expectations we call "culture." As the social philosopher Charles Handy has said, "True individuality is necessarily social. . . . We find ourselves through what we do and through the long struggle of living with and for others."

A narrow vision of what defines you—labels of the past: "I'm the son of So-and-So," "I come from a place called . . . ," "I'm a _____ at IBM"—does not encompass the breadth of your life or your possibilities and potential. It can prevent you from connecting to your higher purpose.

This trap is all too common. I'll never forget the chilling comment from a college senior applying for business school: "Dr. Albion, I've played soccer all my life. The season is now over, and I'm not going to play in the pros," she stammered as her eyes filled with tears. "I don't know who I am."

The Sufi say, "Wisdom tells me I am nothing; love tells me that I am everything. Between the two, my life flows." Business schools provide you with one culture, one way of looking at who you are and how to be a successful person. It is your job to look outside those four walls and inside your own heart. Ask yourself, "How would I define myself as broadly as possible?" Think broadly!

You now have three lifelines to guide you and nothing to lose. If you need help, think back to all the ways you might have defined "who I am" at various ages. Then compile those definitions and see what you have. In the next chapter, we'll complete your self-examination by making explicit the goals and priorities of your personal destiny plan.

Destiny Plan Questions

▶ When people ask you who you are, what do you say? Consider different variations depending on the situation and who is doing the asking.

▶ Think about who you are as defined by four different people in your life. What do those definitions have in common?

▶ Without your current job or family, who are you? Think as broadly as possible about your definition.

CHAPTER 2

WHAT DO YOU WANT?

Success is getting what you want.
Happiness is wanting what you have.

Warren Buffett, famed investor

Like the Mexican fisherman in the Introduction, do you know what the good life is for you? Do you know what you want, and is what you want what you *really* want? Figuring out what is important to you can be hard to do—unless you are someone like Rick Stewart.

Rick Stewart cofounded Frontier Herbs (today known as Frontier Natural Products) in 1976 to fill some basic needs: he wanted some healthier products and hoped to make $5,000 so he could backpack around the world. He earned it, left to travel, and returned to the company until 1999.

Even as the company grew well beyond what he ever imagined, Rick stayed clear on what he wanted from Frontier. He was "underawed" by the company's inclusion in the *Inc.* 500 and its National Small Business Association award but elated by its three years on *Working Mother* magazine's list of the "100 Best Companies for Working Mothers." What were Rick's personal ambitions? "To get my organically grown backyard mowed before it rains again, preferably by one of my four teenage children."

Rick's life philosophy on wants and needs offers a simple equation to get you started on the road to fulfillment: life is about your H being bigger than your W. If you want to be happy, what you have (H) should be more than what you want (W). So you have two choices: you can work to have a big H, or you can live to have a small W. What worked for Rick is having a small W.

Is your H greater than your W? Underlying this question are three considerations, each expressed in the next three lifelines. First, you need to be clear about your wants so that you know what success looks like to you. Second, the role of money in your life is so crucial that it should be examined separately. It's often the elephant in the room that no one mentions. Finally, priorities shift, so it's important to be aware of what yours are and honor them in what you do.

MBAs usually have a big "W". That's part of the business school experience. Business school is Success Central. Parades of CEOs speak in your classrooms and auditoriums about how successful they are. Your school walls are filled with digital information on the world of commerce, who's buying what for mega-millions and who just went public and made a killing. Today, your walls also reflect success in the social sector, like Wendy Kopp and Teach for America. But the "success" message remains loud and clear.

Once you graduate, you start seeing the names of your former classmates in the *Wall Street Journal*, the *New York Times*, and business magazines, one success after another. The implied values reinforce your school experience. At a fifth or tenth reunion, you'll see posturing that reinforces the success story. Being clear on what you *really* want is tough, particularly for high-powered MBAs. It's important to remain connected to who you are and your inner needs that may have been drowned out by the noise of business school.

An "I Want" List from Youth

As I've said, what we really want is to be loved and respected, to have intimacy and admiration. We want a little fun and adventure, too, as we all dream of noble purposes. To get started, ask yourself, "What do I think about in my dreamtime?" Dreamtime takes you back to the questions of Chapter 1 that help you get in touch with your childhood aspirations.

I'd like to share with you an "I want" list through the eyes of a seventeen-year-old who was still in touch with her inner child. It's as remarkable a list as she was a person. I believe you have a list like hers inside you, too. Her list may help you find yours. Note how in her list, she uncovers what she really wants.

Her name was Michela Harriman, a close friend of my older daughter, Amanda. Michela loved to make films, play tennis, and laugh. She lived her life out loud. She wrote the following five-hundred-word essay for college admission. She finished this first draft on Sunday, August 14, 2005, and then left her parents' house to drive to see a friend. It was the last time anyone would see her. Michela was killed in an automobile accident.

Michela's Essay

Some days I say I'm going to be a filmmaker. Not the kind who wears a tight low ponytail topped with a beret and a beaded eyeglass chain around her neck, and sits and stresses all day with a script in her lap.

I want to be the writer who travels to Tanzania in East Africa, lives in a village for a few months and creates films about life there so the rest of the world can glimpse this hidden place.

I want to be the filmmaker who listens to the grief of Afghan women who wonder why no one ever asks them what they want. I want to hear beautiful and tragic stories and tell the world what we are doing right and what needs to change. I want to make films that impact people—make them cry or laugh or shudder.

Some days, though, I just want to curl up under a blanket with a bowl of popcorn and watch the latest Angelina Jolie movie.

Some days I want to be Editor-in-Chief of a fashion magazine. The kind who lives in a penthouse on the twelfth floor in Manhattan yet only uses it for closet space to hold my gifts from Oscar de la Renta, Zac Posen, and Narcisco Rodriguez. The kind who lives on coffee and Power Bars through a whirlwind of fashion shows, parties, and layouts. Or maybe the one who sits on a sunny porch filled with exotic plants, listening to New Age music and dirtying her hands with her kids while they finger paint.

I want to lay paper out on the floor and splatter outfits across the pages placing blues and reds and yellows together but not before meticulously planning where each splatter should go and its size and shape and color as if I were finger painting with my children who are trying to do the same. I want to let my pages tell the stories of powerful women and dainty beauties.

I want people to look at what I create and be influenced by it for an hour, a week, or forever.

Most days I want to be a pop singer, get hair extensions, and find a dog that is able to fit into my clutch. But then I remember I can't dance.

And then I want to be a filmmaker again, because by using my own direction, I can become a fashion editor or a rock 'n' roll chick, or anything else I wish to be.

And in my own films I can leave this world for a moment if it becomes too noisy or crowded or scary. I can fall in love when I'm lonely or be loved when I'm forgotten. I can talk to that someone I miss or change a part of the past I regret.

I think maybe it's freedom I want above all else. And I think that filmmaking and the make-believe that comes with it is a good place to start.

Michela's list resonates with me because I, too, value freedom. When I look back at my path, it is clear that freedom is arguably the most important "I want" on my list. Yet before I read her list, I might have neglected its importance.

Measuring the Good Life

When I ask MBAs, I consistently hear that first on your list—and the main message of your future eulogy (you hope)—is that you want to be thought of as a good person and to have a good life. I can't define "good" for you. What I can do is share with you four metrics I've used with MBAs to construct a simple model that serves as a personal inventory of your goodness and the good life.

The four metrics are service to the community, to the dollar, to the family, and to the soul or self—or as I call them:

Mother Teresa (*service to the community*)
Donald Trump (*service to the dollar*)
Martha Stewart (*service to the family*)[1]
Deepak Chopra (*service to the soul or self*)

---

[1] I know that Ms. Stewart went to jail in 2004 and is divorced, so feel free to pick Julia Child or anyone else! I'm sticking with Ms. Stewart.

The model works on a scoring system, from a low of 0 to a high of 10 on each metric. Score yourself, total the numbers, and you'll have your personal assessment. Of even more interest is how each metric and the total vary over time.

In 2007, I scored myself a 10, 0, 3, and 4, for a total of 17. It was pretty clear what I needed to work on. So far in 2008, I'd give myself a 6, 4, 5, and 8, for a total of 23.

You can see my adjustments, although the bank helped me get the message before I used the metrics! It's also a fun party game and good to do with your partner.

Discussing these scores with students, we evaluated totals as follows:

Under 10: Are you still breathing?

11–20: You need to do some work.

21–30: Not bad, but you're not going on *Oprah*.

31–35: Are you being honest with yourself?

36–40: You are on *Oprah*. Move over Dr. Phil!

MBAs can have fun, too, even if renowned management expert Tom Peters alleged that there's a sign at the entrance to Harvard Business School that says, "No smiling allowed." I think he's just jealous.

Fun is an important part of success. The next three lifelines will help you deepen your understanding of how fun and other aspects of your life are dimensions of what is important to you that you need to make explicit in your destiny plan.

Destiny Plan Questions

▶ Is your *H* greater than your *W*? Explain how you measure each.

▶ What do you think about in your dreamtime?

▶ How do you define being a "good" person? What does the "good life" mean to you?

▶ What does your "good life" score tell you?

Know How You Measure Success

My father believed that a man's success is measured by how much money he makes. My mother came from a wealthy family and focused in her earlier years on status. It seemed that all our cousins and Mom's friends were "big" something or others—doctors, lawyers, CEOs, and so forth.

I certainly didn't fall far from the tree. In fact, a few years ago at a Red Sox baseball game, after I finished telling a story in which I reeled off at least five famous people I'd met, Mom commented, "Mark, if you are so interested in associating with these kinds of people, maybe you should instead try to be one yourself." I'm still learning from Mom in my fifties.

Life is another teacher. I always dreamed of having a book appear on the *New York Times* list of best sellers. When I found out I did, I was excited. But when did I really feel successful, when did I feel I was living the good life?

It was an evening the summer before the book was published when I looked at the finished manuscript for the first time as a whole. I decided to read for a few minutes and see what it was like.

Two hours later, I was still reading. I had tears in my eyes. I was so proud. No matter what anyone thought, I'd done my best. I connected with this work, birthed from someplace deep inside me. I pledged that whether the book sold one copy or one million, I'd be satisfied. I could control my work but not its sales.

I forgot that pledge at times throughout the year. Today, I realize how important it is not to lose that truth. The success is in the work. The joy is in "having written," in knowing that you are "a writer." That experience helped me begin to look in other places, inner places, places where I felt really good about my work, regardless of the opinions of others.

Writing has led to many insights into in my relationship with success. One Sunday night after I'd finished reviewing the galleys of my 2006 book, we were having a family dinner—a rare but treasured experience.

At times I feel underappreciated. I took this evening's dinner as an opportunity to make my feelings known. In particular, I started whining about the fact that no one seemed to read my articles and books, "which support this family." I want feedback, I said, but what I really wanted was a few pats on the back.

Unlike her father, my then eighteen-year-old daughter, Amanda, understood all of this intuitively. After my grumblings reached their zenith, she responded: "Dad, you should know that even if you won the Nobel Prize for your writings, I wouldn't love you any more than I already do."

Amanda knew what I needed to hear. What else is there to say? We all want to feel that our lives have mattered, that we've made a difference in our world. That world starts with our family and friends. It starts with having done something that has positively affected them and their lives.

Success is personal. Success is multidimensional. When I'm asked how I measure success, I call on years of searching to see it holistically. I call on the words of Michela.

For me, success is doing what I believe I was born to do. It is that feeling of being on your destiny path, of having a vocation, a calling, not just a career.

On a daily basis, success means I've chosen to create a life that allows me to live my values every day. Some days I'm more involved with my children, wife, parents, or siblings. Other days I have the *freedom* to help out at my temple or to spend the day quietly writing. In my world, I have one boss, one judge in whom my faith resides. (Of course, I also have my wife of nearly thirty years and two teenager daughters.)

For most of you, service will be a big part of your success and ultimate happiness. Positive psychology researchers like Professor Todd Kashdan of George Mason University further distinguish between "feeling good," which creates a hunger for more pleasure (academics call it the "hedonic treadmill") and "doing good," which research shows leads to lasting happiness. When psychologists contrast the results of experiments in which students do something that gives them pleasure and then perform an act of selfless kindness, the research shows that it's the latter that has a profound effect on happiness, that "doing good is good for you."

So how will you measure success? What's *your* measure, the metrics you'll use in your destiny plan to know if you're on track or off? The risks for

MBAs are that your perspective may be distorted by your business school persona and that being achievement-oriented can cause restlessness. You find it hard to enjoy "success," hard to be as Warren Buffett said, *content*.

I'll conclude this lifeline by sharing a mirror with you that will facilitate self-examination. It's a look at a measure of success from the experiences of a European Net Impact MBA. She was in Costa Rica and met a twenty-four-year-old man named Danly who was working for a local rafting company. They were talking about the environment, Columbus, and general philosophy when Danly said, "Before I stopped smoking, if there was a second life, I wanted to come back as a nonsmoking me. Now that I've quit, I just want to be me."

He said that he had good family and friends, a job he loved, and a rich community life. Working as a rafting guide with little formal education, Danly was "one of the most thought out, knowledgeable, and provocative people I've ever met," she observed. He made only about $60 a day most days, but he still got to travel the world with his job, meet interesting people, and learn different languages and customs. What more could he want?

But it was his statement about wanting to come back in a second life as himself that really shook this MBA. She asked herself, "How many MBAs are that happy with themselves and their lives?" Her response: "I think very few. That struck me as being profoundly sad. If I couldn't answer the question with 'me,' then what am I doing wrong? How would you answer it?"

If there's an MBA trap, this is its root: *measuring success*. What measures mean something to you? And of utmost importance, what role will money play in those measures?

Destiny Plan Questions

- ► How do you measure success on a daily and annual basis?
- ► How do or did your parents measure success? How have their measures and those of business school and your peers affected your notion of "success?"
- ► What would you change about yourself if you could? Why?

Money Doesn't Talk, It Swears[2]

The evangelist Billy Graham once said, "If a person gets his attitude toward money straight, it will help him straighten out almost every other area in his life." I'm always reminded, with a little chuckle, of the following story when I reflect on Reverend Graham's quotation.

A successful MBA banker parked his new Jaguar in front of the office, ready to show it off to his colleagues. As he got out, a truck came along too close to the curb and completely tore off the driver's door of the Jag. The man immediately grabbed his cell phone and dialed 911. In minutes, a policeman he knew pulled up. Before the policeman had a chance to ask any questions, the MBA started screaming hysterically. His Jag, which he had just picked up the day before, was completely ruined. After he wound down, the policeman shook his head in disgust and disbelief.

"I can't believe how materialistic you MBAs are," he said. "You're so focused on your possessions that you don't notice anything else." "How can you say such a thing?" asked the MBA. The policeman replied, "Didn't you know that your left arm is missing from the elbow down? It must have been torn off when the truck hit you."

"My God!" screamed the MBA. "Where's my Rolex?"

Funny, yes. Revealing, maybe. It's like all the lawyer jokes, but it remains a public perception of MBAs, too, though you and I know that it is not an accurate depiction of many MBAs today.

I want to reiterate that my philosophy is "Money *and* . . ." Money can be very good. It's all about how you make it and what you do with it. I love the expression that money's like manure. If you pile it up, it stinks, but if you spread it around, it can do a lot of good. After all, if money doesn't help you find meaning, what good is it?

---

[2] This line is from "It's Alright, Ma (I'm Only Bleeding)" by Bob Dylan, copyright © 1965, 1993 by Special Rider Music.

The challenge of money enters every part of your life and affects your spiritual search for meaning. (A powerful speech on the challenge of money appears in Resource (following the Conclusion of this book. It is discussed in more detail in Chapter 4.) It is a critical element of your destiny plan, though often relegated to a lesser role than it really plays in your life.

Money and meaning, how can you accomplish both? You know that money can't buy meaning, but money doesn't have to change your values, either. It can give you the freedom to express your values and increase personal fulfillment, too.

For example, when Robert Fulghum made millions from *All I Really Need to Know I Learned in Kindergarten,* he made a few small purchases, but primarily, the money allowed him to deepen his relationships with all the nonprofits to which he'd been giving his time. Now he could give them money, too. The real value of money is not in its possession but in its use.

Money and happiness? Research studies in 2006 from Harvard and Princeton indicate that "the difference between making $5,000 and $50,000 a year is dramatic, but the difference between making $100,000 and $100 million is negligible, almost nonexistent." Still, you need enough to cover your basic needs. The Pew Research Center's 2006 report found that 49 percent of respondents with family incomes over $100,000 said they were happy, whereas only 24 percent with family incomes under $30,000 felt the same.

We all need money. The only way to not think about it is to have "enough." So how much money is "enough"? How much does the good life require, Mr. Trump?

Over the past eight years, I've asked about sixty-five hundred MBAs how much they feel they need to make after graduation, either as a single person or part of a couple, to get by decently. Using cost of living indices, the normalized range for this annual amount, for feeling "basically happy," has been $25,000 to $450,000. The median response, however, is well into the six figures; $25,000 is an outlier. Whatever your number, the question is, "How will it affect your options?" The higher the number, the fewer your opportunities to get on your destiny path.

I think it's also important to ask, "What is money?" To me, it is something I trade my life energy for. I remember the old Jack Benny skit vividly. Benny played the penny-pincher to the hilt. In the skit, when an assailant points a gun at Benny's head and shouts, "Your money or your life!" Benny asks for a moment to think about it.

Whereas you might figure out a way to make money while you sleep, if nothing else, your consciousness will be focused on money. That's your price, an oft-forgotten externality of money.

You risk looking at the world in ways to make your money, spend your money, protect your money, invest your money, and so on. How much time do you spend each week on money? The poet and the photographer see the world in their artistic way; the politician sees votes; and the businessperson sees the world through the lens of money. When you set a goal related to something, like money, your price is that your attempts to reach that goal will influence who you are.

That's your risk, mitigated by the power of how you use money. In March 2008, Professor Elizabeth Dunn of the University of British Columbia and Professor Michael Norton of Harvard Business School released their findings on ways money could buy happiness. They performed several studies, primarily with Americans of modest incomes.

The research showed that whereas most people feel they will be happier spending money on themselves, the greatest increase in happiness came from the act of giving. Other research has also confirmed that when you give to others, your serotonin level (a happiness neurotransmitter) rises, as it does for the one accepting the gift and also for anyone who observes the act of giving!

Your challenge is to come to terms with how much money you really need, which depends on what you are going to do with it and what you have to give up to get it. Business school is most concerned with how to make money; little time is spent on what to do with it.

So in your drive for success, will money control you or will you control it? As Jay Gatsby replies in F. Scott Fitzgerald's 1925 classic *The Great Gatsby* to the comment, "I hear you lost all your money in the stock crash": "Yes, I lost every penny in the crash … but I lost all that was important to me in the boom."

I've been there. I've let money control me. The following incident occurred at the time of my twentieth high school reunion. May you learn from my experience.

I left well before the reunion ended because I'd gotten a phone call from a lawyer I knew to do expert testimony out of town at "whatever you want to charge for one day." I was making good money at the time, but I figured, why not add another $10,000 to $15,000 on top of that? I could always see my former classmates later, I thought.

I prepared that evening and left early the next morning to meet with the lawyers who took me to the courtroom. But at the end of the day, I had yet to testify. They told me to stay another day and assured me I'd get paid for that day, too.

Two days turned into three. I was really going to clean up on this one! Including preparation fees, I was looking at a cool $50,000. But it was the dinner with three lawyers the second night that I'll never forget.

We relaxed as drinks flowed, talk drifted, and jokes flew around the table. But as the jokes continued, they became more disturbing. The smile left my face. Within a few minutes, it was clear that these guys were racist, sexist pigs. Putting down women was the initial subtext, but quickly the jokes shifted to people of color. I knew that if I weren't there, they'd probably be onto Jews next.

What should I do? Tell them to shut their traps, give them a stern lecture, and leave the dinner table? That's how I felt, my blood at a boil at this unacceptable behavior. I didn't expect to change them, but I could disturb them. And I didn't have to accept it, even tacitly.

What did I do? Nothing. I didn't say a word. I certainly didn't laugh or join in. I took a few sips of my drink and shut up, waiting uncomfortably for the jokes to stop, for the topic to shift. Why? I'm ashamed to say it, but I wanted the money. I was afraid that if I walked out, I'd be off the case and probably not get paid.

I never did testify. When the client heard from the lawyers what my per diem was, he told me to leave *now*. In the end, I never got paid for the three-and-a-half days, only half a day. I got what I deserved. As the industrialist Andrew

Carnegie warned, "The amassing of wealth is one of the worst species of idolatry. [There is] no idol more debasing than the worship of money."

That's what money can do. I wasn't prepared to deal with a conflict of values. Acting shamefully, I'd lost my integrity. Never again, I promised myself. Money is freedom—the freedom to do special things, not a freedom from anything, not an excuse to hide. I learned the hard way how important it is to keep your priorities clear and act on them, the subject of the next lifeline.

Destiny Plan Questions

► How much is enough? How much money do you need each year to have a decent standard of living? How much to retire? What is the impact of those numbers on your options of what you can do?

► What are you willing to give up to make more money?

► What do you see as the biggest risk in your relationship with money?

■ LIFELINE 6 ■

Don't Treasure Your Trash and Trash Your Treasures

It's easy to lose your way, to fall off your destiny path by getting too caught up in what seems to be important and neglecting what really matters to you. It's all about knowing your priorities and living them.

At my twenty-fifth college reunion (where I stayed until the very end!), I saw a classmate whom I'd just read about in a *Forbes* magazine cover story. He and his business partner looked great on the cover. The story highlighted that they had just sold their business for hundreds of millions of dollars, each owning 50 percent. I gave him a big hug and my hearty congratulations. He thanked me graciously and asked if we could find a quiet spot to talk. We did. He then told me: "Mark, my best friend from childhood and I built that business together from the ground up, but we had disagreements before the decision to sell. Once the sale was finalized, he said he never wanted to speak to me again. I've been heartbroken. To make matters worse, my wife and three daughters barely saw me all those years. Now they just treat me like a one-arm bandit, talking to me only if they want money. I lost sight of what I really wanted out of life, and now I wish I could change it, but I can't."

I gave him another hug and talked with him throughout the reunion, observing just what he said about how his family treated him. As you may have guessed, his wife subsequently divorced him, and he and his daughters are estranged.

The most difficult challenge you face may be how to move a career forward without leaving a family behind. You see success as multidimensional, including a good income, good job, good family situation, and often children. As a recent MBA graduate told me, "Dr. Mark, my dream is to raise my children to be economically successful enough so that they can afford the therapy required to get over me."

Tongue in cheek, but this woman understands how driven she is and how difficult her achievement orientation makes it to live all parts of the good life—at least at the same time. She has experienced how the arc of life, culture, and subliminal societal voices can draw you away. You concentrate on your work, in which you are replaceable. Yet the only place you're truly irreplaceable is at home.

High achievers can get sidetracked in subtle ways by not appreciating what they have and always putting their energies into what they don't have. As the Polynesians are said to query, "Are you standing on whales fishing for minnows?"

You don't need another in-depth discussion about work and family. You know how difficult it can be to get that right. You do need to make your priorities clear in your destiny plan. You can use the four "good life" metrics introduced earlier in this chapter. Score yourself on where you are now and where you'd like to be. Your plan then includes how you will make the necessary transitions.

Beyond work and family issues, I'd like to share with you two work examples that can upset your priorities, often without your even realizing it. MBAs are particularly sensitive to both. The first is the mantra of growth. The demands of growth can push you to create work that is not aligned with your life goals and priorities.

How many times do you think the MBAs I mentor ask me for help in building a *smaller* company? Yet after I hear about their frustrations at work, desires to spend more time with family, or health problems from overwork, we almost always find a way to shrink the company, become more profitable and easier to run, and often have *more* impact on industrywide social challenges.

In fact, the majority of small manufacturing companies I've seen have this problem. The drive to get to 100 percent capacity forces them to push employees and orders, often not from the best customers. This only leads to more pressure, lower morale, and cash shortages. We find ways to reduce operations to, say, 75 percent of capacity, keep the good clients, and relax the atmosphere. We reconfigure the value chain by reassessing implicit assumptions about how the business needs to operate. The result is a better-run, more profitable, and more fun-to-work-for company.

Service companies can run into the same problem, often driven by the need to increase revenue per employee. An MBA colleague came to me after she had cancer. As she realized from growing her marketing measurement company at all costs, "Volume for the sake of overhead is lousy. It will destroy your culture."

She'd run her six-year-old company at $80,000 revenue per employee before the cancer. Her new business model outsourced aspects of her service that were not her unique expertise and reduced her travel time by 80 percent. It ran at half the volume but, within two years, at $180,000 per employee.

MBAs think "grow, grow, grow," not "shrink, shrink, shrink." My own final MBA finance exam was the first case study I'd seen that required us to develop a financing plan to shrink the company. When the professor later became my colleague, he told me that 90 percent of the class never saw the "twist." Students "automatically" developed financial plans to grow the company even though it was in serious trouble.

As with most professionals, you've bought into the cultural stereotypes about what it means to "move forward," about what success looks like. Bigger is not always better. Better is better. It's the same with careers. The second example is the mantra of promotion, what I called in Chapter 1 the Paul Principle.

Many of my friends in their fifties who remain in investment banking have done so by "depromoting" themselves: *stepping down* from management, back to doing deals, something they always enjoyed doing. Others with careers in industries ranging from foundation work to consumer products have not taken promotions to continue doing work they enjoy, avoid moving their family, or get really good at what they do. MBAs are impatient, but today, more realize that by staying in a position longer, personal satisfaction can grow.

The key is not to follow Wall Street's demand for the bright light of growth but to follow the *right light for you*—the right size that fits only one, you, and your destiny plan. The same applies to keeping your career priorities straight: know how you like to work, and do it *your* way.

I had problems choosing what to do and not to do as a Harvard Business School professor. I remember a concerned senior professor asking me about my priorities. He was the course head for first-year marketing. Thirty-two at the time, I was working hard on a case study, which I'm proud to say is still being used at business schools twenty-five years later. However, it led to an important disagreement.

He felt I was spending too much time helping students outside of office hours. He asked what I'd do if "you're working on that Suave shampoo case, which tens of thousands of students and executives will read and learn from, and a student knocks on your door." I said that I'd put down my work and help the student. He explained that I had given the wrong answer. The student could be asked to come back during office hours, and my "important" case study would be finished sooner.

He was right in everything he said. But unlike my submission to the other advice I'd gotten during my Harvard days, I realized that this piece just didn't fit me. I'd spend hours helping my students beyond marketing, with their lives, nurturing the seeds of what would eventually become my vocation. Unconsciously, I was valuing what was important to me and what success ultimately meant to me.

I'd like to conclude this lifeline and this chapter with a comment by someone who had his priorities straight. A few years ago, I met a Nobel laureate in his late seventies. He was friendly, a good listener, and of course, smart. It must feel great to be recognized for a life spent contributing to humanity. And who could argue with that measure of success, of feeling special? I asked him how it felt to win the Nobel Prize. His reply: "It was very nice. It provided funding for important research we were conducting. But you know what really made me feel special? I grew up in Brooklyn, New York, on the fourth floor of a brownstone. Every day, when I returned from school at 3:00 P.M., my mother would be at the bottom of the stairs with a glass of milk and a freshly baked warm chocolate chip cookie for me. *That* was special."

You are special. Using these first two chapters as a guide, you should now have a deeper understanding of yourself and what you want. It's time to bring you into the marketplace, with some cautionary advice to ease your way on your destiny path.

Destiny Plan Questions

▶ Looking at the four metrics you used at the beginning of the chapter to assess the "good life," how would you rank them in terms of priorities? Are you spending your time in a way that honors that ranking?

▶ How would you handle a values conflict with your employer? What personal values are inviolate?

▶ How might you shrink the demands of your career yet have more impact?

Chapter 3 ■ ■ ■ What Can You Do?

To fulfill a dream, to be allowed to sweat over lonely labor, to be given a chance to create, is the meat and potatoes of life. The money is the gravy.

Bette Davis, legendary actor

I can't tell you how many high-ranking executives say to me, "Mark, I wish your MBAs would come to us with an understanding of who they are and what turns them on. I wish they would say, 'Here's what really interests me, here's what I want to do, and here's how it will help your company.' It may take them longer to find the right fit, but when they do, it will be the right job and the right hire."

What can you do? *Anything.* That's a big help! So then, what do you want to do with the life energy you've been given? Can you describe your dream job, the one with no exit plan? Whether you want to start an enterprise or work for one, that dream job needs a description based on who you are, what you want, and how you will add value for your customers or employers. It's a description of how and why you will bring *all of you* to work and be committed to its success.

This process takes time. Pressed for time by your schoolwork and the mad rush of on-campus recruiters, it's easier to passively go along with the established process. But even if you aren't trying to form an alternative plan, it's useful to get down on paper that job description, the core of what I've called your *destiny description,* as I showed my description in Chapter 1.

The work of Chapters 1 and 2 was inwardly focused. Self-actualization, learning how to serve yourself, is a big step for most of you. Chapters 3 and 4 have an external focus. They offer guidance for bringing your dreams and desires into the marketplace of your life. This chapter is more cautionary in tone: keep your values up front, don't get stuck, and don't delay. Its purpose is to give you the greatest opportunity to find your path, stay on it, and get back on it more quickly when you fall off. Chapter 4 guides you by highlighting three critical aspects of a fulfilling destiny path—a path that will twist and turn many times. After all, what is a "typical" path today?

Careers are constantly under construction. Planning is important, but as the saying goes, if you want to give God a good laugh, tell her your plans. Career paths are more of a walkabout than a walk straight ahead. You will craft yours not so much as a single-minded quest but more like grabbing a little of this and that to make a patchwork quilt.

Take the résumé of a friend of mine, Barbara Waugh. She was a faith healer, psychic, bodyguard for the black militant Angela Davis—and holds a PhD. She was the head of worldwide personnel for Hewlett-Packard Laboratories, went on to start HP's bottom-of-the-pyramid business unit, and today heads the company's University Relations division.

In the meantime, Barbara also helped create the vision for the entire 120,000-person company, changing its focus from being the best *in* the world to being the best *for* the world. This is just part of how she re-creates her job at Hewlett-Packard, rewriting her destiny description to focus on issues of inclusion (the poor, people of color) that get her jumping out of bed each morning. It's also Barbara's unique way of adding value for HP.

A road like this does take longer than a conventional path. It can be harder to find a job, but when you do, it will be the job that's right for you. It's a path with stops along the way connected only by your passion and values.

The example of Barbara's road reminds me of how people thrive when they love what they are doing and don't give up when things don't work out because their work connects so deeply with their dreams and desires. It's something I once forgot, only to be reminded by a venture capitalist.

It's Your Will More Than Your Skills

After three years of experimenting, we got lucky: My partner, Paul Birnholz, and I had come up with a "killer product" and a retail channel ready to add millions of dollars in sales to what had been a "hobby" company.

Applebrook Farms was originally housed at my childhood friend's farm in Westford, Vermont. In 1990, we launched our pet products company primarily to give us an excuse to spend time together. Eighteen months later, our all-natural Moon Over Vermont* rain forest dog biscuits took off.

In 1993, a national hotel chain became interested in carrying our two-ounce "pocket paks" of rain forest dog biscuits. We'd need money to increase production capacity and working capital. Fortunately, a venture capitalist told me he'd put up $3 to $5 million. Animal lover Paul didn't want to run the company. We had a great business, so why not me?

At the venture capitalist's office, I gave my best presentation. When I'd finished, he looked me straight in the eye, put his hand on my shoulder to show his respect and friendship, and said to my face, "Mark, I wouldn't give you ten cents. You sound like one of your MBAs. I hear the *finance* but not the *romance*." He acknowledged the importance of strategy and execution skills, but making a young enterprise a success is "more about your *will* than your *skill*. It's how you get through the tough times." He didn't sense that personal commitment. He told me to sell the company, find something I was passionate about, and then come back for funding.

It was a powerful teaching moment. Venture capitalists care as much about the people as about the plan. And this venture had the wrong people: *people without passion*. In fact, the one-third of my start-ups that have been successful began with the weaker products and plans but the right people. Yet when do you ever talk about the *romance* of business instead of the *finance*?

Career success is often the result of your will more than your skills. A corollary, however, remains important: that to carry out your will, you need to rely on leveraging your strengths instead of compensating for your weaknesses. You have to *want what you have*. I believe that you can spend too much time trying to become well rounded rather than choosing work environments that suit you already.

For example, I'm not good at business politics but excellent at inspiring people on an infrequent basis. If I wanted to work for a large organization, however, I'd need to be much better at politics and dealing with people daily. So I don't work in a large organization, and even in my own organizations, I've learned to stay away from the main office. I visit, do my rah-rah stuff, and then get back to advising clients, speaking, or writing, keeping me out of trouble and working on what I love.

Leveraging Your Strengths to Serve

Paul Orfalea provides another example of employing this strategy in a business that deeply reflects his passion for service. Paul had a learning disability that wasn't diagnosed as dyslexia until he was well into grade school and far behind his classmates. It was a humiliating period for him, years of low self-esteem and not knowing where he might fit in. Paul finally completed junior college, but what could he do to earn a living? What did he have to offer an employer? Not much, he concluded.

Thirty years later, Harvard Business School profiled three entrepreneurs who had built brand-name businesses and made a large impact on society. Two were from the MBA program. The third, Paul Orfalea, had merely attended an executive program. What had happened in those intervening decades? In 1970, Paul had founded and then as CEO for nearly three decades built a multibillion-dollar business service organization called Kinko's, an American staple sporting his nickname (Paul had "kinky" hair).

Paul created a business where operational efficiency depends on recognizing spatial relationships, service needs and business trends. He couldn't read well and didn't work on it, instead observing, talking to people, and listening to just about everything and everyone.

Taking a city walk with Paul is an unforgettable experience. He sees something here and there, and *voilà*, he synthesizes them into a new business concept! Because he spends little time reading—but knows every number in the business—and spends all his time making sense of human nature, he continually reinvents this process. It's his special gift and the basis of his creativity. It also means that he depends on others for what he can't do and appreciates their doing it, enhancing his service ethic.

Managing Your Risk-Reward Trade-Off

The difficult part for most MBAs is that once in place, this path must remain focused on how to serve others. I've observed that it can be hard for MBAs to do this, primarily because it seems that the more people have, the more they expect in return. So it requires that you understand that if there's a return on your serving others, it often comes over long periods of time and *not in ways you expect.*

In Paul's case, his expectations were low. When people came to work with him at Kinko's, "I was so happy to have them. I thought everyone was smarter than me and how lucky I was that they were here." He also was obsessed with service to customers and coworkers.

One day after several store visits that uncovered costly inefficiencies in Kinko's checkout systems, I asked Paul how Kinko's was able to remain financially successful. He responded that the company depended on frontline coworkers' being educated enough to help each customer, whatever the needs. "If we give coworkers everything they need, then they will do the same for our customers." Paul believed that personal service, not technical systems, were the heart and soul of Kinko's success.

Paul's service ethic grew out of an iron will born of a background of feeling incompetent and worthless, an ethic that grew deeper over time. I remember when we first met, he invited me to his home for dinner and apologized before we sat down, knowing my reputation: "We should do more for the outside community, Mark. I know that. But I'm more focused on making sure our twenty-five thousand coworkers can put braces on their children's teeth and send them to college." Those who serve the most want to do more. It's how they express their values and turn them into value.

Destiny Plan Questions

► How will your destiny path be able to integrate serving others with serving yourself?

► Describe your dream job. What would you need to do to attain it?

► Take a look back at your career to date. What constants do you see among your various jobs?

► What do you see as your biggest strengths? How do they support your passion and future success?

■ LIFELINE 7 ■

Turn Your Values into Value

We all dream of noble purposes. Often for conflicted achievers like myself—who accrued money and status but not through work that we find most meaningful—the opportunity to bring our values to work is what we've been waiting for. You can bring your values to work as an investment banker or a Peace Corps volunteer, but the best time is as early as possible in your career. Ironically, the higher up you are on an organizational chart, the *less* opportunity you have to do something new. You have greater responsibilities and expectations, so that deviations from your prearranged script are difficult at best.

How you turn your values into value depends on how you like to spend your time and use your strengths to support your passion and your ability to serve. To understand how to add value, it helps to ask questions about how you like to work and work best, for example: Do I like to work by myself or with others? Do I like a fast-paced environment? Do I like to persuade people or offer a balanced point of view?

How you add value better than anyone else in your own unique way is best done by first being clear about what you *don't* do. For example, you can tell if a company has a clear strategy and follows it if the company divests itself of profitable businesses. If businesses don't fit the company's values and its creation of value, it's better to sell them off now before they dilute energy and become unprofitable. What activities should *you* divest? Then you can ask,

"How can I add value in a unique way?" The answer is by having what you do reflect you, of course! Your business, your career, should be an outgrowth of who you are and what you want.

I'd like to share with you a four-step process for creating value, which I've developed over the past decade working with MBAs at large companies. Many of these people are frustrated, feel they're smarter than their bosses, and are impatient to either move up or get more ideas implemented. Each step requires a service orientation: you must look at your project from someone else's point of view. That means you need to reduce your decision maker's risk in allowing you to go ahead, and initiatives that can lower costs are more readily implemented than those that project higher revenues.

1. *Make the business argument.* You want to bring your values to work? Figure out how they might help the business, keep the company ahead of competitors (or regulators), or at least not cost the company money.

For example, an MBA in at an investment bank was allowed to buy $20,000 of recycled paper for the main office. She looked at the current use of paper, calculated how many documents could be printed on two-sided paper, and estimated the savings from using smaller margins. Then she measured the results. "I had to show that we'd spend no more than $20,000." What's measured is what matters, essential to get values implemented and to sustain them.

Here's a Kinko's example. At one time, coworkers knew that Kinko's was going to raise outside money but not how or when. Paul wasn't in a rush. I surveyed coworkers and found that they were each spending about four hours per week talking with coworkers about the impending change instead of working. At an estimate of $10 per hour for twenty-five thousand coworkers, I showed Paul a bill at the end of one week for $1 million—the cost of lost productivity. A decision on how the money would be raised was made within days.

2. *Build a constituency.* If one person wants to do something, that's nice. If a group wants to do it, that's a *movement.* Put together a small group within the company that supports your project. You also have many minds to tap for ideas, and it's more fun to do things with peers and pizza. It may be difficult to

get senior people to join publicly, but many will support you behind the scenes once you reach a critical mass. Do your work outside of office hours.

3. *Make your boss look good.* Keep your boss posted on what you're doing, when you're meeting, and so on. Ask for reactions within a set time period, with the understanding that if there's no response, you have the green light to proceed. It's also helpful to find out what's on your boss's agenda and how you can make your boss look good to your boss's boss.

At Net Impact, MBA students who are involved in initiatives to change curriculum at business schools understand that it is helpful to get support from alumni. They give money to the school and hire graduates. That support helps the department chair bring student proposals to the dean.

4. *Understand company politics.* This is the number one failing of MBAs (and myself!). Learn how initiatives get approved and put into action in your company. As much time as is spent on the business argument, probably more time needs to be spent here. It helps to have a mentor within the company who can guide you, especially if you're new.

When I served on faculty committees, different kinds of initiatives involved different school politics. For sizable capital expenditures, the dean was usually looking for a rubber stamp from the committee. In hiring new faculty, senior faculty relied on the recommendation of young faculty members who were more knowledgeable of new research methodologies.

This four-step process also applies to starting your own business. Let me share a story about a small man with a big impact, Joe Shurdut, and then highlight the four-step process. Uncle Joe believed that everyone was equally deserving of opportunity, a value that made him a multimillionaire.

As a young teen in the early 1960s, I spent part of my summers at Aunt Fay and Uncle Joe's summer home in Hyannis, Massachusetts. Actually, I didn't visit a particular home. They owned *streets* of homes around a lake! The homes were always full of Filipino guests, and Uncle Joe's jokes, followed by laughter, filled the air. He always had a warm hug and a hearty laugh for me.

I didn't know them that well, but I knew that they were wealthy. I'd been told that they had made their money in the Philippines as the owners of one of the largest American businesses in the Pacific. I recently learned the details when I ran into the son of a Filipino man who had worked with my uncle. He was excited to tell me the tale.

In 1933, in the depths of the Great Depression, Uncle Joe and Aunt Fay looked abroad and settled in the Philippines, which at the time was a U.S. territory. Uncle Joe started a business as the exclusive distributor for International Harvester heavy equipment in the Philippines. For eight years, he built a healthy business and made a good living, with a unique compensation system, particularly for those times and with Filipinos.

"Your uncle treated us like family," I was told. "He was truly kind. He took no salary himself during the year, and at the end of each year, he would take 50 percent of the profits for himself and distribute the other 50 percent to his coworkers." He kept the financial books open and spent many an evening teaching his coworkers how to understand balance sheets, income statements, and cash flow statements, as well as sharing what he knew about the business itself.

Then World War II came, and the business closed. Uncle Joe was taken prisoner and interned in a labor camp. He survived, but as a skeleton. When the war ended, he returned to the United States. It would take him five years to recover his strength enough to work again. The business was long gone.

He and Aunt Fay, now penniless, decided to return to the Philippines and see if Uncle Joe could find some of his former coworkers. He was concerned how they were doing and hoped to start the business again. "Do you think he started the business again?" my storyteller asked. "Yes," I anticipated. "Not exactly," he replied. But did he find his coworkers? "Yes, he did."

When the war ended, his Filipino coworkers had found one another and started the business up again by themselves. They had accomplished quite a bit, too.

Circumstances were so bad after the war that they took the opportunity to acquire *all* the other heavy machinery dealerships as well. Thus they became the sole distributors of all heavy equipment in the Philippines. And over the course of the five years, at the end of each year, they had put away 50 percent of the profits for Uncle Joe, whom they *knew* would return. Uncle Joe was a multi millionaire. "Your uncle spent the rest of his years [he died in 1969] building the business with his 'family' to great heights and doing whatever he could for his people and his adopted country, the Philippines."

Here's how the four-step process applies to the story of Uncle Joe:

1. *Make the business argument.* Uncle Joe trained coworkers to understand how the business created value. *Everyone* could make the business argument for a new initiative.

2. *Build a constituency.* When a group of coworkers completed their training, they then taught new coworkers.

3. *Make your boss look good.* Uncle Joe talked of what today we'd call an "inverted management pyramid." He was at the bottom, with his coworkers at the top. And with their unusual knowledge base, all coworkers looked very smart to potential clients.

4. *Understand company politics.* Uncle Joe developed a strong culture with clear politics, the politics of respecting and caring for one another. And as you saw, they cared for him the most.

Turning your values into value is easier when you work for a company with values similar to yours or are able to create your own company culture with your values. When a values conflict exists, research indicates that most MBAs do *not* leave their jobs—at least not right away. But if you are thinking of leaving, it's easier to walk if you keep your walking costs low.

Destiny Plan Questions

▶ How can you turn your values into value? How do your values make you more valuable to your company?

▶ To focus your energies, what things should you *not* do?

▶ In going through the four-step process, apply it to your answer to the first question. For example, can you make the business argument for bringing what you care about to the workplace?

Keep Your Walking Costs Low

Why do some MBAs pursue their dreams while others live with dissatisfaction and unhappiness and do nothing about it? Why do some change jobs if they are unhappy while others do not? What is holding them back from following their passions? After all, if highly educated business school students can't live a life that's more than money, who can?

President Kennedy once said that we should not let our fears hold us back from pursuing our hopes. That sentiment encapsulates this lifeline, which is at the heart of the risk-return trade-off and central to embarking on a destiny plan. Think of all those MBA "buts," those excuses that stop you from making the changes you'd like to make, from taking the daring adventure called life. You feel trapped.

It's hard to leave what you know to find what you love. When do you make a big career change? As I noted earlier, you do it when the pain of not changing becomes greater than the fear of changing. The easier it is for you to recognize that you're in the wrong place, to decide to make a change, to make it and then to sustain it, the better. The lower your walking costs, the less you are committed to a situation, the less fear and perceived risk you feel, the greater the return from a career well chosen, and the easier it will be for you to leave. Symbolically, this is

$$\textit{Pain of no change} \; > \; \textit{fear of change} \; = \; \textit{change}$$

Rather than increasing your pain, let's identify the risks and carefully weigh their importance. That helps you lower your fear of change.

There are two caveats. Often MBAs don't give a job enough time to find out whether it's a good fit. Intel's cofounder, Andy Grove, once said that he wouldn't hire MBAs because it took six years to find out if you could be good at product management, and no MBA would wait that long. MBAs can be impatient. Conversely, you might not leave when you'd like because of a commitment to colleagues or a project. That may be true for a while, but as time passes, you're fooling yourself. A walking cost is controlling you.

There are three types of walking costs, three types of risk that can make you feel trapped. They are economic, performance, and psychosocial risk.

Economic risk measures your financial concerns, which may soon be "Who's going to pay the mortgage, tuition, and country club bills?" In choosing a job after graduation, you worry about paying back your school loan. If that stops you, you're stuck before you start. MBAs mention this concern the most. It is the *least* risky of the three walking costs.

As noted, money concerns often cover up our deeper desires to be loved and respected. I can't tell you how many MBA spouses, typically the wives, say, "I wish he'd talk to me and realize that I just want us to be happy. We don't need all those things. But we do need to have some fun and create a fulfilling life together." Research indicates that at least in the early stages of careers, MBA women are more connected to their values than men.

Performance risk measures your résumé concerns ("If I fail at this, will anybody want to hire me again?") Or maybe you have only worked at one place all your life and don't know if you have any value anywhere else ("I'm 'good' here, but will I be good anywhere else?"). "I'll probably fail," you might think, "or at least not be as good, and then what?" So you look for a way to continue doing what you've been doing instead of growing into new opportunities.

As MBAs, you're used to being good at what you do. That need to be successful right away can preclude taking advantage of opportunities to grow. Trying something new can be hard. You may not be very good at it at first and decide not to do it even if you'd like to learn. Guess what? Whenever you make a big change, such as going from finance to a marketing position, you'll start at the bottom of the ladder. That allows you to build a good foundation, however, and keep you on your destiny path.

Psychosocial risk measures identity concerns. This third walking cost is often the pernicious troublemaker behind the other two. It taunts, "Who are you? I thought you were a big shot, but you're actually a little shot." It's your status in the eyes of the Joneses. Change challenges your identity. How can you lose the role everyone expects you to continue to play? That's why it's important to start your four-question personal planning process with who you are and what you want in order to be comfortable in your own skin.

My friends tease my wife about her choice in marrying me. In front of Joy, they challenge me: "Joy married this highly successful Harvard guy. You were supposed to make a lot of money (*economic*), continue to move up in the world (*performance*), and have a Beverly Hills lifestyle (*psychosocial*). You're lucky she's still with you!"

Let me share with you my exit from Harvard to illustrate these three walking costs. First, I was making a very good income, not just as a professor but also as a consultant and company owner. I was worried about replacing that income stream. Next I had the performance risk of how it would look on my résumé. I was leaving a great job for a chancy start-up. If it failed, what would it mean when I went looking for my next job?

Most difficult was that once I left, the screen went blank. I wasn't getting calls to deliver high-priced speeches or do executive teaching and consulting. I was no longer "Mark Albion, Harvard Business School professor." I was just "Mark Albion." Loss of a prestigious identity can be emotionally challenging.

So how do you deal with these three risks? First, it's important to control the controllables. Things happen in life. But if you spend your time worrying about how other people act, you're wasting a lot of energy. As the saying goes, you can't direct the wind, but you can adjust the sails.

After Harvard, we economized and moderated our lifestyle so that the financial impact would be less severe. In terms of performance risk, no matter what you do, if you do it with honesty and integrity, people understand. In 1993, I cost investor friends into the seven figures when my biggest start-up went belly up, but I communicated with them all the way, told the truth, and took a bigger hit than they did. Those relationships have led to many business opportunities the past fifteen years.

Perhaps most important, today's world *expects business failures* on your résumé; otherwise, you're simply not trying hard enough. It's said that if an entrepreneur has one success in one try, it's luck. But two successes out of ten tries, that's good! Failures can in fact make it easier for you to get hired or raise money. Business failures are the best learning experiences—once you've recovered from them.

I was careful about psychosocial risk. My wife and I had a social life separate from Harvard. I had friends who knew little about my association with Harvard and couldn't have cared less. "They'll let anyone teach there, won't they?" was their reaction.

After I was profiled on *60 Minutes,* my longtime friend Bob Maclay gave me a call: "Saw you on TV tonight, Albion. Good show. That bald spot of yours has really grown." Harvard or not, these relationships help you through life and give you the strength to let life's intangibles trump the tangibles.

The more experience you have walking, the easier it gets as the risks seem smaller. As Kenny Moore, a former monk and currently the corporate ombudsman at the energy giant National Grid, said after running a company funeral to simulate the effect of deregulation on the company, "What did I have to lose? Not much. Just the respect of my peers." In his life, Kenny had survived two near-death experiences. Worrying about losing a job, money, or standing in the community seemed negligible by comparison. That's why you shouldn't wait too long if you sense it's time to move on.

Destiny Plan Questions

▶ What fears are keeping you from pursuing your hopes? Use the three types of walking costs to structure your answer.

▶ What can you do to reduce your perceived risk, your fears of changes you'd like to make but haven't made yet?

▶ Along your destiny path, what are the things you can control and the things you can't? How will you deal with what you can't control?

Don't Live a Deferred Life Plan

After speaking at Harvard Business School one afternoon, Warren Buffett was asked a question that made him chuckle heartily. He clearly had been asked this question many times before. "Mr. Buffett, what I'd like to do is go out and make a lot of money for about ten years and then go and do what I really, really want to do. What do you think about that?"

With that wry smile he sports, Buffett paused for a moment, took a measured breath, and spoke slowly in his best midwestern drawl: "Sonny, it sounds to me like you're saving up sex for old age."

Are you living a deferred life plan?

Think about it. You'll spend about one hundred thousand hours at work. Ten thousand hours of that you'll spend rebooting Windows. But those other ninety thousand hours? Shouldn't you have fun and find fulfillment beyond simply getting a paycheck?

I can't count the number of times MBAs tell me of changes they want to make, things they want to do, but they are waiting for ... something! "I'd like to do it now but ..." and then "I'll do it when ..." A cliché because of its truth, life isn't a dress rehearsal. Don't worry so much about your life ending; *worry more that it never begins.*

Other excuses include "My spouse won't ..." or "I need to make this much money for my children." Have you talked to your spouse or children about what they want—for themselves and for you, too? Spouses usually want to see you happy. Children want you stress-free and want to learn your values. Is it worth it to make the money to send your children off to college when the price is not knowing them before they leave? Is deferring your life plan what you want to teach them?

Any plan, no less a destiny plan, needs a timeline. No time ever seems like the right time, but trust me, the right time is now, if not yesterday. That's because almost every MBA I've talked to after making a big change only regrets that it didn't happen sooner.

To ensure that no one is living a deferred life plan, that no one dies with one's music still inside, is Kenny Moore's pet project. "Years ago," he confesses, "I had the good fortune of being diagnosed with 'incurable' cancer at its most advanced stages. When I came back to work, I decided it wasn't worth waiting to try to be who you are."

Kenny gave up climbing the corporate ladder and decided to rearrange his priorities. He spent his time being authentic and contributing to the corporate good, to the good of others. At work, he spoke his mind more, took more risks, and developed a greater sense of humor.

"One advantage to surviving terminal illnesses is that you don't really care about outcomes. At the end of the day, if I was still alive, I considered it a success. The monks call this 'holy indifference.' All you do is make sure your intentions are pure and then move forward. No concern for 'ambition,' for moving up the corporate ladder. Who has time for that? Just do the right thing and help others."

The result of his holy indifference? Kenny kept getting promoted! He says he felt like he was being given a Zen career lesson: *You only get to keep what you give away.*

"What I've come to realize is that the best thing I ever did for my career was to forget about having one. To focus on what needs were not being met and then try to serve them. To not leave my deeper self behind just so I could make it in the world of work but instead to bring all of me to work, all my values, for better or worse."

This lifeline challenges you as you write your destiny plan. You don't need to make dramatic changes all at once. Many MBAs find that small, incremental steps move them along their path just fine. My transition from consulting to writing was done first on weekends only. Then I took a couple of months to write a book, and a few years later, writing became my primary vocation.

How do you know when it's time? I've found that when you start asking a lot of people about making a change, especially strangers like me, you're probably overdue.

The former president and owner of the Vermont Bread Company, the largest woman-owned business in Vermont, Lisa Lorimer had spent her entire adult life building the company when she decided to sell it. I asked her why. "I'd lost the 'yippee' factor," she said. "After all those years, I woke up one morning and knew the excitement was gone. It was time to move on."

A destiny plan is not built around your search for success but around your search for what brings you the greatest joy—the kind of joy I believe you will find through service to others. You'll know when it's time to move on. Because if what you are doing isn't fun anymore, why do it?

Destiny Plan Questions

▶ Are you living a deferred life plan? Explain.

▶ Does Kenny Moore's "holy indifference" apply to you or not? Explain your answer. What can you learn from Moore's perspective?

▶ To make changes in your career, how do you feel about small changes versus dramatic leaps? What factors would affect how dramatic a change you might make?

CHAPTER 4 ■ ■ ■ ■ ■ WHERE ARE YOU GOING?

Far away, there in the sunshine are my highest aspirations. I may not reach them, but I can look up and see their beauty, believe in them, and try to follow where they lead.

Louisa May Alcott, famous author

You've now come nearly full circle. You began the search for your path of service with the end in mind. Reflecting on your eulogy and your lifetime contribution right up front should have helped you set a course on your personal strategic plan, what I've called your destiny plan—your moral compass for career decisions.

I've shared my belief that it will be your acts as citizens, as servants to society and to those in need, that will make you feel fulfilled and for which you will be most remembered. I've shared my belief that the purpose of life is to stand for something, to make a contribution. What a joy it is to embrace that one thing, that one contribution you will be remembered for! To do that, it really isn't important what your skills or position in life are or what the market says it wants. What is important is that you find the path that makes you come alive.

In that light, there are two speeches I wish each of you could hear. The first came from the chair of Paul Newman's Hole in the Wall Gang camp. He gave the Saturday morning keynote at the Net Impact Sixth Annual National Conference at Yale School of Management in

1998. The camp was founded ten years earlier for children with cancer and other life-threatening illnesses. With four hundred MBAs packed into the chapel, he read letters from some of the children.

Throughout the speech you could have heard a pin drop. It was one of the most moving experiences of my life. The window into these children's lives and the gratitude they had for the camp expressed in those letters touched everyone present in a way that rarely occurs in business school. As I left the chapel, I thought how this kind of speech can have a dramatic impact on the way you approach business school, your career, and your legacy.

The second speech appears at the back of this book as a resource. Titled "The Challenge of Money," it was delivered on Earth Day 1995 by Elliot Hoffman, cofounder and CEO of specialty baker Just Desserts, to 350 members of the Social Venture Network. It was a speech from the heart, an open letter to that community about the values we live versus the values we say we live, our relationship with money, and our relationships with one another.

Elliot questioned who we are and what we need to do differently to get where we really want to go, which he summarized as follows: "We're looking for a quality of life having little to do with material wealth. We're all desperately searching for intimacy with each other, with ourselves, and with the natural world. We can do that in our own ways by making the world a touch better."

Elliot and his wife, Gail Horvath, founded Just Desserts in 1973. It became a San Francisco landmark, renowned for its community service and humane workplace as much as for its cakes and coffee. Presidential candidates made campaign stops there to praise it as one of our finest models of capitalism. Elliot became a business hero, alongside his friend Ben Cohen, of Ben & Jerry's fame. When he joined the Social Venture Network in 1992, Elliot was SVN's most sought-after CEO in the United States.

Elliot and Gail took a sabbatical in 1993–1994 to spend a year devoted to their two children. When they returned to work, new competition had squeezed business. After eighty profitable quarters, they were looking for money for the first time.

Read the speech, and reflect on the values you're expressing and the legacy you're creating. Also notice how the speech touches on all three lifelines in this chapter: the importance of making a difference to even one person, the personal and social value of developing a supportive community, and the satisfaction of being involved in social challenges that will not be met in any one lifetime.

What happened next? It would take six years, but Elliot and Gail raised enough money to build their manufacturing facility in an enterprise zone in Oakland. The facility opened in August 2001, just before sales tumbled in response to 9/11. Bad timing. On July 3, 2003, Just Desserts filed for Chapter 11 bankruptcy protection for reorganization.

Elliot got cancer, lost a kidney and almost died.

The speech is forceful by itself, but when you know what happened, I think it takes on an even greater power and raises even more questions. With Gail as his partner in work and at home, Elliot exemplifies the values espoused in this book and by our socially responsible business networks. How can someone so well intentioned and so successful by any definition of that values-laden word go under?

Five years later I had an answer. Elliot got up and began again, creating New Voice of Business, a nonpartisan membership organization whose mission is to awaken, inspire, and mobilize the power and creativity of business. New Voice supports businesspeople to play a positive leadership role in addressing the core challenges and opportunities of our times. Beginning with California's AB32 solar legislation, New Voice has achieved success more quickly than he could ever have hoped.

As he continues to make the same kinds of contributions to society and his community *in a new form,* he is having an even greater impact through New Voice, built on his thirty-year reputation with Just Desserts. (He is also the chair of the Presidio School of Management.) The phoenix rises again.

When I reflect on my time with Elliot and Gail, I think of our conversations. Coded with our values, our conversations are about what needs to be done to make the world a better place and how what we're doing will, we hope, be part of the solution. It's the conversation of *citizens,* a perspective burned into my memory by a publisher from Barcelona.

In 2002, I went to Barcelona, Spain, for a week of speaking engagements for my latest book, which had just been published in Spanish. I met publisher Jordi Nadal—poet, philosopher, and global ambassador of kindness and compassion, conveyed with warmth, wit, and intelligence. We found that we had much in common and shared our views night and day. But it was during an early-evening talk about our children that Jordi posed a question that I reflect on nearly every day. In response to the question "How are we raising our children?" Jordi asked, "Are we raising our children to be consumers or citizens?"

We live in a producer-consumer culture. Citizenship may be something you devote yourself to . . . when you have the time. As you go through the last three lifelines to complete your destiny plan, ask yourself, "In which direction am I headed, *consumer* or *citizen*?" To start, you need only look at your impact on one person at a time.

Destiny Plan Questions

▶ What did you learn from Elliot Hoffman's speech, and how does it affect your destiny plan?

▶ Do you need to feel connected to a social cause in order to make a difference? If not, what might take the place of such a cause in your life?

▶ Reflect on your daily conversations, primarily at work. What values and life perspectives do they reflect?

▶ Are you more of a consumer or a citizen? Explain your answer.

■ LIFELINE 10 ■

Look Not at the Masses but at the One

When I think of someone who had a positive impact on thousands in need, I think of Mother Teresa. She never let the vastness of the suffering, the realization of billions in poverty, stop her. In her words, "I never look at the masses as my responsibility. I look at the individual. I can only love one person at a time. . . . So you begin. I began—I picked up one person. I wouldn't have picked up 42,000. . . . The same goes for you. . . . Just begin." I needed that advice fifteen years ago.

I've always thought of Net Impact that way: changing the way we do business one student at a time. But I haven't always acted that way.

In the early days of Net Impact, I never knew whether I'd have five or a hundred people at my sessions. Some schools had established chapters, but most were struggling. That's why I was excited to speak at the Columbia Business School. Our NI chapter president, Jared Goldstein, was a rabid NI devotee and a relentless promoter of the cause.

I arrived to find the auditorium packed and the doors wide open to accommodate the overflow crowd of people standing in the yard outside. The several hundred people in attendance generated an energy that led to one of my best presentations. The following day, I read with pride several school write-ups on the speech as well as a short piece in the *New York Times*. I was flying high.

Later that day, I spoke at New York University's Stern Business School. We had a small chapter but a good time slot, which usually guarantees a good crowd. Eight people showed: two friends and six students. I ditched my speech and invited everyone to sit in a circle with me at the bottom of the amphitheater-style classroom. We had a thoroughly enjoyable two-hour career conversation.

Today I am in touch with not a single person from the Columbia session, but I know all the people from NYU. And I believe I've helped them find career fulfillment. At which speech did I have the bigger impact?

MBAs get caught up in numbers. The MBA tone is about doing something "big." I too have fallen into that trap, writing about being "great" and addressing big causes connected to bigger stories and bigger impact. Instead, follow Mother Teresa's focus on "small deeds with great love" and one person you can help, someone whose spirit you can uplift, whose suffering you can alleviate. As it is said in the Jewish Talmud, if you save one soul, it's as if you have saved the world.

When you design your destiny plan, it's helpful to visualize that one person or one situation you can change for the better. That's what Kenny Moore does to "awaken joy" at National Grid. It's work so important that he's one of the few employees who report directly to the CEO. Let me share with you an illustration of Kenny's work as a purveyor of happiness, resulting in increased corporate productivity. (You need that business argument!)

Kenny's favorite children's book is Eileen Spinelli's *Somebody Loves You, Mr. Hatch*. It's a story about the impact you can have on people when you help them feel appreciated and recognized for making a contribution. That's a way anyone who wants to serve can do so.

Mr. Hatch is an isolated working man whose life is turned around by an anonymous box of candy left at his doorstep with a note reading "Somebody Loves You." That incident touches him so deeply that he dresses up more nicely, greets strangers, and becomes a magnet for children. Lots more happens, so get the book, read about his ups and downs, and delight in the ending!

After reading the book, Kenny decides to bring Mr. Hatch to corporate America! He anonymously sends a $40 floral arrangement to two unsuspecting managers each Monday morning. A note is attached: "Don't ever think your good efforts go unnoticed." Signed: "From someone who cares."

He designs a program, does pilot studies, measures results, the whole bit. Just when he's ready to spill the beans to a corporate senior vice president (who had received a "Mr. Hatch Award" floral arrangement), the SVP stops him to say how much that anonymous bunch of flowers meant to him. He was thinking of early retirement but now is reenergized to focus his time on mentoring individual employees. "I know it's impractical. After all, we've got thousands of them. But I'd like to give it a try."

Kenny's self-effacing assessment of the anonymous program after the first year: "Have I changed our corporate culture? No. Was I able to get everyone together, tell them the business plan, and demand that they implement the Mr. Hatch Award? Heck, no." But he says he does look forward to coming to work Monday mornings, a small number of employees go home Monday night with a smile or a quizzical look on their faces, and coworkers are having a blast trying to figure out who's sending flowers, what for, and how come. Some may be dreaming of getting flowers themselves!

Kenny's "Mr. Hatch" program demonstrates how one random act of kindness for one person can not only touch that person's life but affect others as well. And others, and others, until an entire community is affected. Even the community surrounding your community can be uplifted. It's not about size and scale. Purpose is infectious: from one person to another, from one community to another, and the world changes.

Destiny Plan Questions

▶ How do you think about and measure your impact?

▶ What obstacles do you have to overcome to have your desired impact?

▶ What "small" deeds can you do to increase someone's feelings of appreciation and contribution? Consider one specific person as an example.

■ LIFELINE 11 ■

Surround Yourself with a Community of Love

To follow your destiny plan, for support when you're down or lost, to accomplish what you want to accomplish, and to experience the joy of work, you need other people. A small work community that supports you is also a community, a company, that is more likely to contribute to a kind world as well, not just on earth but in heaven, too, as the following story relates.

What is the difference between heaven and hell? Both initially look the same to a new "recruit": a wild party in a large banquet hall with plenty of men and women, food, drink, and song. The difference is that in hell no one is smiling. Everyone has to eat their food with utensils that are so long it's impossible to lift the food into one's mouth. Unless they grow longer arms, they'll go hungry. But the utensils are no problem in heaven. Each person is feeding the person across the table.

I love the expression that we are all angels with one wing, able to fly only when we embrace each other. Being in a community like "heaven" produces a lot of energy and happiness. Is that good for business?

One summer, I did a research project with an investment bank to look at how we could predict which retail companies would be the best investments over the next five years. The number two factor was what you'd call a "touchy feely" factor. It was a feeling you got when you walked into the home office. The top-performing companies had a buzz of excitement in the air, of people working *together* on projects that engaged them as individuals and as a team.

When I hear from MBAs who are happiest with their new places of employment, their number one reason is that they enjoy the community of people at work. Starting with their boss, they soon learn that if they are complaining about colleagues, suppliers or clients, something is wrong. It's not that you should *love* everyone, but respect, trust, and a sense of fairness at work are good places to start. And who wants to be lonely in the midst of community?

Conversely, when you look at your current work with the end in mind, you may not like what you see. Are you in the "right place" for you? It's important to look at where a career decision may take you. Look around at the senior people in your company or potential employer. Whom do you want to most be like in twenty-five years?

The wife of a Colorado environmental entrepreneur and MBA lecturer asked him that question several years ago when he began his career as a corporate lawyer. "Which of the partners do you want to be like in twenty-five years?" His response? "I don't want to be like any of them. They're all boring, fat, divorced alcoholics!" He resigned two weeks later.

Nowhere is that community spirit more evident than in South Africa. Beyond starvation and the tribal atrocities you see in the news of Africa, South Africa's unique gift to the world may well be the spirit of *Ubuntu*. In Nelson Mandela's tribal language (Xhosa), one of eleven official languages in South Africa, "*Ubuntu ngumntu ngabanye abantu*" is roughly translated as "a person is [can only be] a person through other persons." Or as some like to say, "I am because we are," first mentioned in Lifeline 3.

Ubuntu puts others before oneself, but does so in a way that helps each person reach his or her full potential. By doing the best for the community, you end up doing what's best for you, too. As Taddy Blecher, CEO of CIDA, a university system run on *Ubuntu* principles, says, "It's not by looking only after yourself that you work for the good of everybody. It's by looking after everybody that you ultimately create the basis of wealth for yourself."

How might the concept of *Ubuntu* fit into your destiny plan? Let's look on a business operated on the principle of *Ubuntu* so that you can see the humanist philosophy in action. It will help you reflect on the role of community in your career.

I spent a week teaching at a South African business school where every week, a group of thirty students go on a field trip to visit a nearby business and offer consulting advice. This day, I joined them on their trip to a small hotel and restaurant owned by Joe Mugabwe (not his real name).

We traveled by bus a few hours north of Johannesburg. As we got closer, the scenery became browner and poorer. Yet as we neared Mr. Mugabwe's place, we passed an oasis in the desert: a primary school that had been recently renovated. It was ... stunning. And so were the children, dressed in brand-new school uniforms playing on first-rate playground equipment. Excitement to see Joe's place grew.

In a few minutes, we got our first look at Joe's hotel and restaurant. How shall I explain? Well, have you seen the original Hitchcock thriller *Psycho*? If you remember the Bates Motel, *that* was the Ritz Carlton compared to Joe's place! It was that bad. Creepy bad. The MBAs immediately started scribbling down notes.

We arrived and walked into the lobby to wait for Mr. Mugabwe. The inside décor matched the outside. The torrent of student notes continued. Mr. Mugabwe came out and greeted us warmly, sat down, and smiled, awaiting our questions.

With some hesitation, a student asked the obvious first question: What is your turnover [sales revenue]? "About one hundred thousand," Mr. Mugabwe replied modestly. "One hundred thousand rand per year. That's not bad for a small place like this," responded another student. At the time, a rand was worth about one-sixth of a dollar. Almost sheepishly, Mr. Mugabwe corrected the student, "No. I'm sorry I wasn't very clear. I meant one hundred thousand *U.S. dollars per month.*"

The students gasped. Notebooks were filled with more scribbles. A loud buzz now permeated the lobby as students whispered excitedly to one another. After a pause came the second question: What's your margin. "Oh, I'd say it's about 70 percent." This was met with loud whispering; I overheard comments like "What's he doing with all that money?" and "He must have a boat in Cape Town."

After an uncomfortable silence, there was only one question left along this line of inquiry: "Mr. Mugabwe, what are you doing with all that money? Would you like us to help you use it to fix your place up so you can increase turnover and profitability, if that's possible?"

What was Mr. Mugabwe doing with all that money? Not taking the best care of his hotel and restaurant, obviously. I think you now know the answer. In fact, after a few moments everyone in that lobby knew. Remember the school we passed?

OK, but what about future proceeds? Rather than respond verbally, Mr. Mugabwe took us into a back room that housed a drafting table. On the table were the plans for a regional technical school. After the students graduated, they could then get training for good jobs.

We could do a case study of how this worked, but let me just point out a few things to guide you in your career search for work that matters in a community you care about.

People staying at the hotel and eating at the restaurant knew where their money went. Few complained about any lack of services or niceties at the place. In fact, customers would often help out, fix things, make beds, and the like during their stay—and leave a little extra money, too. Whereas Joe had funded the school, other members of the community paid for all the children's clothing. So where else would anyone stay or eat in the area if not here? After all, this hotel and restaurant was theirs, too. It was inseparable from the community.

The question remains as to whether *Ubuntu* will work in a modern-day capitalistic society. On my trip, I visited a dozen companies operating successfully in this manner. *Ubuntu* was the company's cultural foundation. However, each had *Ubuntu* in its DNA from day one.

How will you create your own *Ubuntu* community in your career? It might help to know that the Nguni word for work, *umsebenzi,* literally means "service." Compassion is a central part of *Ubuntu.* Africans are known for *ukwenana,* an act of giving or sharing without expecting anything in return. Another practice called *ukusisa* is a form of investment that does not require collateral and also maintains the dignity of a poor person who has no assets.

The starting point for building an *Ubuntu* community is to learn everyone's names. In South Africa, with eleven different languages, meeting this initial requirement is no easy feat. But it is considered the essential first step in recognizing the personhood of another. It then follows how important it is to learn about each person's family and background. The process takes time, but more respectful communication and more rapid implementation of other people's initiatives make up for the time initially spent.

It will take generations to know how South Africa and *Ubuntu* will fare in the twenty-first century. But isn't that kind of timetable true for any path worth pursuing?

Destiny Plan Questions

► What would your ideal work community look like?

► Are you a "responsible" member of your work community? How could you improve?

► How does the concept of *Ubuntu* apply to your career and your destiny plan? Give details of three specific instances.

■ **LIFELINE 12** ■

Plant Trees Under Whose Shade You'll Never Sit

In business school, you rarely encounter a situation where you are setting goals that are lofty enough that they are not meant to be attained, only pursued. Yet that kind of goal can be the engine of your destiny plan.

This thinking is counter to MBA teachings. If nothing else, the executive stock option packages alone increased focus on short-term results. It's said that nowadays, a new CEO has ninety days to show results. Strategic plans are often not implemented. Business focuses on the here and now, the measurable and the doable.

I believe that you're each inspired by lofty goals and their challenges. Bringing them into the heart of each company and the soul of every career gives meaning to your lives. Along the way, a lot of good can be done.

Your destiny plan, therefore, should include smaller, achievable short-term goals that keep you on track and measure your impact, even if your ultimate goal is never achieved. Achievements, however small, should be seen as opportunities for small celebrations to keep the joy and feeling of accomplishment alive in your daily work.

One MBA knew his ultimate goal, eradicating discrimination around the world, would not be reached in his lifetime. But that realization didn't stop him. He wasn't trying to change the world. He just wanted to change *his* world. He concentrated on one part of the world, one country and one action and, if I dare say, one man. He was able to find satisfaction in planting that tree. But to do so, he gave up more than expected for any MBA. Here's his story.

In 1988, Reebok sponsored Amnesty International's Human Rights Global Rock Tour. Led by Sting and Peter Gabriel, famous musicians performed around the world to celebrate the fortieth anniversary of the United Nations signing of the International Declaration of Human Rights. Little did Joe LaBonté know that his involvement would cost him a career but gain him a life. (Is everyone in this book named Joe?)

A few years before, Reebok cofounder and CEO Paul Fireman had hired Joe, then president of Twentieth Century Fox, to step in as Reebok's new president and expand its multibillion-dollar franchise around the world. Joe had gone to night school at Northeastern, a blue-collar city college, and was the only person ever to go to Harvard Business School from a night school. A tireless, dedicated worker, he paid his dues every step of the way for twenty-five years, determined to achieve a better life for his supportive wife, Donna, and their children.

When Amnesty International was looking for corporate sponsors for the Human Rights Rock Tour, Reebok and Nike were having public relations problems in the African American community. And at that time, the eyes of the world were on South Africa and the oppression by the white minority. Symbolized by jailed freedom fighter Nelson Mandela, human rights in South Africa had become a global issue.

Reebok sponsored the entire tour. In preparation, Joe visited South Africa twice, only to return a changed man, a man who *felt* injustice. He didn't understand how this atrocity could exist, how citizens of this planet could allow it to exist. "How could I as a parent and grandparent do nothing about this injustice? How could I explain it to my children, to my grandchildren?" he asked me when we first met.

Joseph P. LaBonté, family man and businessman, had no choice. His mind could not stop what his heart knew. If others couldn't, or wouldn't, stop this oppression, maybe he could. After all, he had always been able to solve any problem he confronted in business. Why not one as important as injustice? The street-tough city kid, who had spent his life climbing the corporate career ladder, had found another challenge. How could he use his platform as president of Reebok to try to make a difference?

Whereas Reebok would continue to support human rights with an annual award program, human rights could not be the centerpiece of Reebok's strategy. Joe needed a deeper involvement. He had to help free Mandela and see black South Africans get a new constitution.

At fifty-four years old, Joe LaBonté gave up his job and all he ever knew for something he believed in. Joe founded American Business to Free South Africa (ABIFSA). He enrolled *Fortune* 50 CEOs to guarantee tens of millions of dollars for South African investment if Mandela were released, apartheid ended, and the constitution changed. He met with Mandela the day after he was freed.

Joe LaBonté had made a difference. He had kept his promise to his children and his grandchildren . . . and to himself. He had planted one tree, though several more would be needed. Joe's involvement led him to return to corporate America as the CEO of another public company. However, now he was known for his concern about the larger issues of life. He left to start his own company, dedicating his time to mentoring the next generation of business leaders to put humanistic concerns at the centerpiece of business lives.

It's said that service to our communities is the rent we pay for being here. If so, what is your service? If I were starting out today, I'd work on educating women around the world. I believe that if all women were educated equally to men, most of the world's problems would vanish, though admittedly we'd have a few new ones pop up! That would be my tree to plant. Just one. And then maybe one other... And perhaps another after that...

Destiny Plan Questions

▶ What "trees" would you like to "plant"?

▶ How can you best balance your short-term needs with your long-term goals?

▶ What are you willing to give up to reach your dream?

■ ■ ■ ■ ■ CONCLUSION: FROM SUCCESS TO SIGNIFICANCE

Do not go where the path may lead, go instead where there is no path and leave a trail.

Ralph Waldo Emerson, poet

What would the world be like if everybody loved his or her job? If when you're at work, you could wear the clothes and be the kind of person you've always wanted to be? You'd be happy and fulfilled. I know you would do a lot of good things to help others. You'd be living your destiny plan.

Isn't that the primary message of *More Than Money*? First, get things right with yourself (Chapters 1 and 2), and service will follow (Chapters 3 and 4)—passion becomes compassion. I hope you will think of what you value above all else. I hope you'll remember your best times at work and how good it felt to work toward an important goal with personal passion and common objectives. I hope you will think seriously about your place in the world and how your talents can be of service.

I believe that the days are past of e-mails ranging from suicide notes to "lost and wandering" by the hundreds each week from MBAs, some of the most highly educated people in the world, living in the United States, a country with as much opportunity as any. The risk aversion and the lack of knowledge even about how to find out what you love and how to pursue it have saddened me.

The challenges are basically money and perceptions, real or imagined, positive or negative, of what parents think you should do. That can be more broadly seen as peer pressure and your struggle, as e. e. cummings put it, "to be nobody but yourself, in a world which is doing its best to make you everybody else, means to fight the hardest battle which any human being can fight, and never stop fighting." It's been my struggle, too, but what I've learned is that you're different. That's where I have hope.

In 2006, I noticed a sea change at business schools around the world. Whereas one northeastern business school may have had ten students interested in microfinance the year before, now it was hundreds. Most schools had new programs in sustainability to respond to skyrocketing student interest not only in microfinance but also in social enterprise, corporate social responsibility, and clean technology. "Sustainable business" became a buzzword in the business community as well. Jobs in these sectors increased dramatically, though still not as rapidly as demand.

What happened is the subject for another book. Social Venture Network member Muhammad Yunus's winning the Nobel Peace Prize for his work in microfinance, followed by former Vice President Al Gore sharing the prize for his work on climate change, are clear signals. But I saw, I *felt*, a new consciousness from your generation. And with the global challenges we face together, *you are the generation we have been waiting for.* You will become a great generation, I am certain.

Yet in these exciting times, I've found little business school support for your inner growth, of equal if not greater importance if you are to handle the world you're inheriting. Your generation may be the first in the West not to be as financially successful as your parents. Nevertheless, my belief is that you'll be the most successful generation at finding meaning in your lives.

In that spirit, *More Than Money* started by asking you to reflect on your eulogy and consider how you will contribute by serving others. Next you worked through the four questions to connect who you are and what you care about to what you do and the legacy you want to create.

On the way, you learned to keep your walking costs down to help you manage your perception of risk, surround yourself with support, and don't put off until tomorrow the somewhat frightening changes that you should make today. Don't worry about making mistakes. Make them with honesty and integrity, and your next job is on the way. And don't worry about what others think as much as what *you* think. Concentrate on controlling what you can control, and let the chips fall where they may. Most of all, have fun. Life isn't short. It can be pretty long. It's too long to get trapped in work you don't enjoy and too long not to get involved with work and people you love.

Of course, you need to be clear about what your personal compass is telling you. That can be hard. But if you don't know what success means to you, if you don't know how much is enough, who does? That's your foundation. It should be as strong as possible *before* you venture into the workplace. You will find out where you fit in by not fitting in and make several midcourse corrections. But as long as you keep your priorities straight, you'll be fine. Build that community around you. It will support you by listening to you speak of your challenges and questions. It will keep you strong. I hope Net Impact can do that for you at some level as well.

Remember Barbara Waugh's path and that a typical career path is always under construction. The balancing act of work and family, of money and meaning, of contribution to others and to self is also not a straight line. As the ancient Chinese proverb explains, to walk straight ahead on the beam of life, first you fall of to the left, and then you fall off to the right. You end in the middle.

More Than Money contains a number of stories about my experiences. Yes, I do like to write about myself. But seriously, my point is to illustrate that I, too, have struggled, like most business school graduates—struggled to overcome the biggest risk in life: coming to the end of your days without being able to say you've lived your life without regret. Fortunately, I found my path, though later in life. It's the path I've called your destiny path. As you know by now, you start your path with the end in mind, by asking yourself, "What will my contribution be?"

I'd like to offer you one last story, which I believe captures the spirit of *More Than Money*. "Sam" was twenty-nine—close to your age—when I met him. He had his MBA from a Canadian business school and had made quite a bit of money in real estate. In the few months that I knew him, he became an important teacher in my life.

I met Sam in Goa, India. We were all hippies back then, fleeing America and Europe in the early 1970s, looking for a better life. Fueled by inspiration from the writings of Kerouac's *On the Road* and Michener's *Drifters*, we were in our early twenties, ready to challenge the world.

Sam was the "old man" at the beach. He had purchased a beautiful home, had a new truck and car, and had plenty of food and drink. He offered young lost souls whatever we needed, from food and drink to transportation to housing.

One day, I heard that someone had totaled Sam's car. What had Sam done? Nothing. It was apparently an accident, but there was no penalty, no apology made. I thought about it for a long time before approaching Sam. But after a month, I couldn't keep it in any longer.

As we were walking along the beach, Sam telling me a story about life and personal philosophy, I stopped and turned directly toward him. "Sam, you've got to stop letting people take advantage of you," I commanded him. Taken aback, Sam could only return, "What do you mean?" "I mean, all these hippies are ripping you off, Sam. They eat your food, drink your beer, fill up your house every night with *their* guests, total your car (I had to get that in!), and what do you do? Nothing. I feel really bad for you."

Sam took a moment to figure out how to say what he wanted to say. "Look, Mark. I appreciate your concern. But there's no need. I'm getting everything I want because I don't 'want' anything other than the opportunity to give to some young people in need. I have no expectations other than to continue doing this until my money runs low, and then I'll return to Canada and make some more. But it is my pleasure to be able to do this."

We spoke about giving and getting more during our brief time together. It was a consciousness I had never experienced. The mere act of giving was all he wanted. As months passed, a community developed around Sam on that beach in Goa. Because of his generosity and uncomplicated "love," the community learned to take immaculate care of his home and future cars.

As the year ended, Sam returned to Canada. I once heard that all great things begin in poetry but end in real estate. Yes, Sam became a well-known real estate developer. But he was known as well for his philanthropy and generosity to all who worked with him as for his business acumen. Maybe you know who he is.

I'll leave you with that question and the following eulogy for Sam, whom I will never see again. After all, this is a guidebook of questions and inspiration.

Thank you for taking this journey with me. I hope you find your place in the world and make it better than you found it, so that indeed, you will see *your* world in your life. *Godspeed.*

To Sam, with love, from Mark:

We'll remember you more for who you are than for what you did.

We'll remember you more for the size of your heart than the size of your wallet.

We'll remember you more for how much you gave away than for how much you made.

We'll remember you as much for your kindness as for your wisdom.

And we'll always remember you for how you loved and how we loved you.

Destiny Plan Questions

▶ What book has had the greatest impact on your life philosophy? (Mine is Daniel Quinn's *Ishmael.*) Make sure you incorporate its lessons into your destiny plan.

▶ Share your destiny plan out loud with a partner or friend. What feedback did you get, and what will be your first step in implementing it?

▶ Have you met a "Sam" in your life? What did you learn?

▶ Can you now be a "Sam" for someone else? Is it time to mentor another?

■ ■ ■ ■ ■ RESOURCE: THE CHALLENGE OF MONEY

Elliot Hoffman

Speech delivered to the Social Venture Network, April 21, 1995

Considering that this is a special day, Earth Day, I will start with a brief quote that my mother related to me just about a month ago. She said, "When the last fish is caught, when the last tree in the forest is cut down, when all the water is polluted, man will finally realize that we can't eat, drink, or commune with money."

I'd say that the greed for money has played a pretty significant role in the degradation of our home, Earth. But no matter what happens, I have faith in Mother Earth, that she will, in the end, take care of herself. Even if it means getting rid of that pesky species, *Homo sapiens*. Maybe, just maybe, we can raise the level of consciousness to a plane that enables us to see a clearer path to fulfillment and a quality of life with each other and our Earth that nourishes, heals, and sustains life on our planet. We will soon see if that's the case.

Gail, my wife and partner, and I have gone through a financial struggle with Just Desserts since our return from my sabbatical last July. It was a real mind-blower for us. It was possible that Just Desserts would have gone away. To me, that would have been a very sad commentary. Not only for Gail and me and our children, but for our community as a whole, along with our 320 staff members.

You see, Just Desserts has been a very integral part of our community, and, I'd like to think, one of those models of business and community responsibility, albeit an imperfect model. For me, the past nine months have been the most stressful in memory. Coming off absolutely the most idyllic year of my life, spent with my family, I moved directly into the year from hell.

Over these months I've experienced the ebb and flow of the feelings of terror, the fear of being broke. How are we going to educate our kids? How are we going to pay the mortgage? What will everyone think? What would we do? Waking up in the middle of the night in a cold sweat, heart pounding, shallow breathing, having to calm myself down. Telling myself, "This stuff could kill you!" And I really love my children and want to see them grow up.

Then there's the other side of it that says, "Let go of the fear. It's all just part of the journey anyway. Look at all you're learning from this. The kids will be fine. They've already had a wonderful start in life. Just Desserts is getting through this tough time. The worst is past. We're getting healthier. You've been a very successful person in so many ways."

Since returning from my sabbatical, I've made a lot of changes, some very painful. We've restructured our company. I've cut people at the top, including a partner that started with Gail and me in our house twenty years ago. She's also a very, very close friend, whose cheesecake recipe started it all.

We have built Just Desserts over the years with no outside capital, all internally generated cash and debt. Now we are putting ourselves back on the path of healthy, profitable growth, and we *will* keep our heart, our soul, and our passion alive.

Money has never been a major focus of my life. I've never had a lot of money, never been poor. I grew up in the Bronx in the '50s. My father had two jobs to support us until 1955, when he was murdered, a victim of a holdup at a friend's clothing store on Jerome Avenue in the Bronx. He died forty years ago last month. March was a very painful time for me.

When my dad died at the age of thirty-one, Mom was left with three little kids. I was the oldest at seven, my brother Neil was five, Debbie was five months. My mom had never worked before in her life. She pulled it together, got a job, and we survived.

Money was not a major issue. We just didn't have much. The values we were brought up with were family, friends, and community. To this day, old family friends tell me about my father and what a tremendous community person he was. Even though he had no money, when the United Jewish Appeal came around for a donation, he gave. When someone was in need, he was there. I'd like to think that my own passion for community is a trait I inherited from him.

Coming of age in the '60s, the human values so close to us then are very much a real part of my own life today. The accumulation of money was something that Gail and I never focused on. My own passion was to create a business that was built on high-quality human values. A place where people are respected for who they are, the quality of the job that they do, and not by their sex, sexual orientation, color, nationality, or any other artificial criteria. It's a company built on great products, a good workplace, and a positive influence in our community.

I think that we've done a lot of good for our fellow human beings, besides making great treats. We spent our money providing fully paid health benefits, fully paid maternity and paternity leave—years before it was even a topic of discussion. We looked to create jobs. I spent lots, in hindsight, probably too much time as an advocate for the small business community. I spent a major amount of time and some money to start and help build the Garden Project, where dead souls blossom. I probably didn't place enough attention on money. I was probably out of balance.

Time, life is going faster and faster for all of us these days. Where are we all going in such a hurry? Losing time, losing life. If I remember correctly, wasn't the era of new technologies supposed to give us more freedom, more time for life and family, more human time? Is anyone having more time these days? Does anyone *know* anyone having more time these days? The old Jack Benny joke—"Your money or your life?"—seems very real. What's life? It's time. I don't care who you are, how much money you have. All we really have is time. We have become a time-impoverished society.

I took time for myself and my family last year. I took a year sabbatical from my business and devoted it to my wife and my young children. I was determined that I was not going to be one of the fathers that said, "I didn't spend time with my children, and now they're grown and gone"—especially after having missed out on my own father. I do not take time for granted. Did the universe slam me for daring to get off the track, even for a brief moment?

I believe that we are not really searching for money. We are all desperately searching for intimacy—with each other, with ourselves, with the natural world. We all know that something is very wrong, yet it's difficult to put our finger on it clearly. I'd like to believe that we are looking for a quality of life having very little to do with material wealth.

I met with a financial guy in the garden at our bakery earlier this month. Some of you know this pretty special garden, where lives grow alongside the vegetables. "Bob," we'll call him, said to me, "You should be very proud of what you've achieved here. Building such a highly regarded business, with terrific brand equity. You've been a model of business and community responsibility in San Francisco. You've done some great things here very successfully."

I said, "Thanks, Bob, that's nice. But it's feeling to me these days that in the end, society doesn't really care about this stuff. It's money, not people." And he said, "You may be right."

Another venture capital guy I met with in the garden last fall, "Joe," we'll call him, was born into one of America's wealthy families. Nice person. In our first conversation he said to me, "We invest in the 'G' word." "Joe," I asked, "what's the 'G' word?" "Growth—fast, high growth. Not steady, solid, but fast, blow-it-out growth," he replied.

In our phone conversation a week later, Joe reminds me, "We invest in the two 'G' words." "Oh," I say, "last week you told me of the 'G' word. What's the second 'G' word, Joe?" I'm sure many of you would guess correctly: "Greed. *We invest in greed and growth*," says Joe. Joe is now compost in the garden.

Is this the reality? Is this what money is for? We've worshiped it. We kill for it. We make war over it. We rape the Earth for it. Maybe it's like good and evil, love and hate. Maybe we've got to have both greed and generosity. Maybe I'm just concerned that we seem so out of balance. Shouldn't we set more boundaries on greed? Who am I to say at what level one is greedy? Do we let it go and trust that there will be self-regulating mechanisms on greed and the devastation it causes?

I don't know the answer. But it seems to me that the real regulator for our greed is our Earth. In the end, Mother Earth will regulate us out of existence as a species if we don't get ourselves under control. It saddens me because I want my children, our children and grandchildren, to have a quality of life that we'd be proud to pass on to them, instead of what we are likely to leave them. As our Native American brothers and sisters said, "We don't inherit this planet from our parents. We are borrowing it from our children."

The financial people I've talked with this past year tell me that the pure dollar return on the investment is the key, if not, only criterion. The garden's a nice touch. It's nice that we provide hope and jobs for people, some of whom had no hope. But it's not really important to money. Never mind that Dwight and Tyrone and Gus are now leading totally productive lives instead of robbing you at gunpoint or doing some serious bodily harm to you, a loved one, a friend, a fellow human being. Never mind that their peers have new positive role models.

How about Forrest Brown, Jr.? A father at seventeen, he never held a job, going down the same road as his father. From the garden to his first job as a bread-baker trainee in our bakery, now he is running the bread operation. A wonderful new role model for his five-year-old son, whom Forrest now has full custody of.

Does money care that Suzie Mendoza has been a fully productive member of our baking staff for over two years now, after spending the last fifteen of her thirty years as a heroin addict and prisoner, losing her first two children to the courts? Does money care that she is a changed woman and leading a new life?

To the venture capital people I've talked with about money, human returns are not really part of ROI. There's no such thing as "ROC," return on community, or "ROH," return on humanity. It's a nice touch, but . . . It's wonderful, but . . .

Financial returns are certainly important. But should they be the sole returns? What about the *s-o-u-l* returns? Are there investors and individuals here and out in the world who believe in and value the importance of multiple returns? A multiple bottom line that includes human, community, and social returns?

Doesn't it make sense to invest money in making our communities better places to live and work? If not, I don't care how much money you have or where you live. You will not be immune from the rising tide of despair, hopelessness, and all the ills that come along with these realities.

Our main bakery is in an enterprise zone in the inner city of San Francisco. We employ people from the community. The garden is right there. I see, feel, hear, and touch people who feel the desperation and have little or no hope. It is real. And we have got to do something about it, or we are all in deep you know what.

There are those of us in business who work hard to improve our communities, who believe that we can make money and we can make a difference in people's lives. Are there those with money who are willing to partner with us in our efforts, willing to play for the long term, instead of the usual "highest and quickest" return? Or is there a disconnect between our relationship with money and our espoused values? Are spirituality and humanity one thing, our money and our investments something else?

Just Desserts has been and will always remain a vehicle for making the world a touch better. As I continue on this journey, one of my goals is to find the right financial partner or partners in the near future. Are capital and spirituality, money and community, financial returns and human returns totally disjointed concepts that are not to be uttered in the same breath? I hope not.

What is the role of money in today's and tomorrow's world? My own belief is that money is a major resource that must be used to improve the quality of life on the Earth and in our communities, to provide hope for a decent future. Is there patient, caring capital out there that would like to join us in our efforts to make wonderful treats, to provide hope for many who have been hopeless, and to work with us to continue building one of those models that helps show the world a new way? And make money, too? We do some great things at our place, and I'm proud of what we've built and what we do in our community. I'm excited about what lies ahead of us and look forward to giving you a positive update on our journey next fall.

■ ■ ■ ■ ■ ACKNOWLEDGMENTS

If you are coming to help me, you are wasting your time. But if you are coming because your liberation is bound up with mine, then let us work together.

Lilla Watson, Australian Aboriginal woman

Authors quip that when you steal from one person, it's plagiarism. But when you steal from many, it's research. *More Than Money* is a research book par excellence!

From whom did I steal, you may ask. Certainly my ideas are not unique—only Adam could speak to Eve without worrying that someone said the same thing before he did. But seriously, I've read many insightful books on this topic and have traveled to business schools on five continents to give seminars on social responsibility, service, and personal fulfillment. Thousands of young MBAs have helped create the content and intent of this book.

I've listened to the concerns, questions, and life stories of those many MBAs, followed by e-mails and phone calls. They have stimulated my thinking of parallels to my life. I have synthesized their wisdom and for the past seven years focused on developing a process that addresses MBAs' career challenges.

I am no guru, no answer man. I'm a fellow journeyman. I've asked a lot of questions and had the life experiences of a fifty-seven-year-old man who continually tries to reinvent himself—"predictably unpredictable," my father called me. Thank you for helping me—and helping me help you.

I'd also like to thank the following:

The Temple Beth David community, who have brought me closer to God.

Mother Teresa, for keeping me on this path when I wanted to leave and for keeping me humble (not always successfully) when I wanted to be arrogant.

My parents, for teaching me what values are and what they are not. My mother, for always supporting me.

My wife and children, for challenging me to be better at the small, "simple" things in life.

Harvard, for giving me a platform to do this work and for making me grow up and find myself.

The Social Venture Network, for giving me a tribe of originals who have many minds but one heart dedicated to creating a world of more social and economic justice.

Net Impact, for giving me hope for the future and contact with a generation of young people who make me proud to be called "teacher."

Contributors to expressions used in the book, most notably Donna Carpenter and Maurice Coyle, who in 1999 helped come up with the four questions and the term lifeline.

Reviewers Chris, David, Doug, KP, Kyle, and Phoebe.

Berrett-Koehler, for conducting business with an eye toward creating a world that works for all and for giving me the opportunity to work again with senior managing editor Jeevan Sivasubramanian, who's always there for me, and editorial director Johanna Vondeling, without whom I wouldn't have done this book. They are the best in the world and the best for the world.

■ ■ ■ ■ ■ INDEX

■ ■ ■ ■ ■ ABOUT THE AUTHOR

Don't be humble. You're not that great.

Golda Meir, former prime minister of Israel

Mark Albion is a social entrepreneur and author. He spent eighteen years as a student and professor at Harvard University and Harvard Business School and was profiled on *60 Minutes* as one of the top young business professors in the United States. He has served as a board member and consultant to major retailers and consumer product giants such as Coca-Cola and Procter & Gamble and has written three award-winning marketing books. He left Harvard to develop a community of service-minded MBAs and cofounded Net Impact in 1993. He has since spoken at more than 125 business schools on five continents, for which *Business Week* called him "the savior of b-school souls."

In 1996, Mark began *Making a Life, Making a Living,*® a five thousand–word monthly newsletter read by students and executives in eighty-seven countries (check it out at www.makingalife.com). He wrote a *New York Times* business best-seller by that name, followed by *Finding Work That Matters* (a set of three CDs) and, as part of the Social Venture Network series, *True to Yourself: Leading a Values-Based Business.*

Mark has been married for twenty-seven years and has two daughters, one of whom is a Net Impact lifetime member. His daughters know him best as the man who rode across Afghanistan on horseback.

What is "The Good Life?"

Watch the 3-minute movie *The Good Life*, written and narrated by Mark Albion, and produced by Free Range Studios. Mark tells the story from *More Than Money* of the MBA and the fisherman, illustrated with beautiful watercolor-like animations. If you like it, tell your friends!

See it here: **www.more-than-money.org**

■ ABOUT BERRETT-KOEHLER PUBLISHERS ■

Berrett-Koehler is an independent publisher dedicated to an ambitious mission: Creating a World That Works for All.

We believe that to truly create a better world, action is needed at all levels—individual, organizational, and societal. At the individual level, our publications help people align their lives with their values and with their aspirations for a better world. At the organizational level, our publications promote progressive leadership and management practices, socially responsible approaches to business, and humane and effective organizations. At the societal level, our publications advance social and economic justice, shared prosperity, sustainability, and new solutions to national and global issues.

A major theme of our publications is "Opening Up New Space." They challenge conventional thinking, introduce new ideas, and foster positive change. Their common quest is changing the underlying beliefs, mindsets, and structures that keep generating the same cycles of problems, no matter who our leaders are or what improvement programs we adopt.

We strive to practice what we preach—to operate our publishing company in line with the ideas in our books. At the core of our approach is *stewardship*, which we define as a deep sense of responsibility to administer the company for the benefit of all of our "stakeholder" groups: authors, customers, employees, investors, service providers, and the communities and environment around us.

We are grateful to the thousands of readers, authors, and other friends of the company who consider themselves to be part of the "BK Community." We hope that you, too, will join us in our mission.

A BK Life Book

This book is part of our BK Life series. BK Life books change people's lives. They help individuals improve their lives in ways that are beneficial for the families, organizations, communities, nations, and world in which they live and work. To find out more, visit www.bk-life.com.

Visit Our Website

Go to www.bkconnection.com to read exclusive previews and excerpts of new books, find detailed information on all Berrett-Koehler titles and authors, browse subject-area libraries of books, and get special discounts.

Subscribe to Our Free E-Newsletter

Be the first to hear about new publications, special discount offers, exclusive articles, news about bestsellers, and more! Get on the list for our free e-newsletter by going to www.bkconnection.com.

Get Quantity Discounts

Berrett-Koehler books are available at quantity discounts for orders of ten or more copies. Please call us toll-free at (800) 929-2929 or email us at bkp.orders@aidcvt.com.

Host a Reading Group

For tips on how to form and carry on a book reading group in your workplace or community, see our website at www.bkconnection.com.

Join the BK Community

Thousands of readers of our books have become part of the "BK Community" by participating in events featuring our authors, reviewing draft manuscripts of forthcoming books, spreading the word about their favorite books, and supporting our publishing program in other ways. If you would like to join the BK Community, please contact us at bkcommunity@bkpub.com.